My Life in Ps

CW01660079

Grangegorman Dublin 1972-2002

Lucy Walshe

Copyright © 2024
All Rights Reserved

No part of this book may be reproduced or transmitted in any form or by any means, electronic or mechanical, including photocopying, recording, or by any information storage and retrieval system without the written permission of the author, except where permitted by law.

I would like to thank my husband for his support and stories in my book, to my three sons,

Mark Liam and Stephen, and my daughter Fiona for their support and encouragement.

For my friends who read my book and gave me feedback, to anyone who helped me publish my book.

It is my ambition to leave this legacy to the next generation.

Acknowledgements

I would like to sincerely thank my husband Billy, my family, and three sons: Mark, Liam, and Stephen, and my daughter Fiona. My friends and colleagues for supporting and encouraging me to write this book, and my friends Cait and Terry, who read the book and gave me feedback. This book is a legacy of what it was like to nurse psychiatric patients in Grange Gorman in the 70s. I, like my colleagues, started nursing at the age of eighteen on a hospital campus of eighty-five acres and a population of 1,600 patients.

I would like to thank all the male and female senior nurses who shared their knowledge and experiences with me, so I too, like they did before me, learned a lot about life and the reality of where we were and what was expected of us.

I treated every patient with respect and dignity no matter how insulting, offensive and dangerous to me. I realised these unfortunate people were ill and not responsible for their actions. However some psychopaths or sociopaths were responsible in some ways for their actions but I still treated them the same too.

I would like to thank all of the organisations, all sports, football, hurling, hockey, soccer, table tennis, bowls, drama, and all of those people who spent their spare time making these organisations work, and to those who showed kindness to us when we felt like leaving the profession as it was a hard one. Those people made life fun and laughter to carry on every day through good times and sad times. We were a rock for each other.

To our unions and committees who stood up for our rights as nurses and patients and the years of negotiations to improve conditions for staff and patients.

For all staff whose stories enlightened me from nurses, doctors, tutors, engineering and ground staff, ambulance crew, OT's catering staff, Chaplin, accounts, typing pool, and administration with whom we had regular meetings.

I hope this book will inspire young nurses to realise that each person is an individual and not just a number, and treat them as if they were their own father, mother, sister, brother or relative, and being in a hospital can be so isolating and cruel. Many older people are not familiar with modern technology or may not even have a mobile phone, so contacting their relatives for them is very important.

Contents

Preface

This is the story of my working life in a psychiatric hospital in the 1970s. It's about my life and the lives of the patients I met and cared for over thirty years.

I am writing this book because I want today's generation of nurses, care staff, auxiliary staff, nurse specialists, and doctors to know what it was like to nurse patients with a psychiatric illness, and many other undiagnosed conditions in the last fifty years, as to why patients ended up in a psychiatric hospital. I loved working in St Brendan's when I got over the shock of how big it was and how it was managed. It was like a second home to me because of the support and comradeship of all the nurses, doctors and auxiliary staff who worked there. If there were good times we celebrated, if there was a tragedy, we were united in grief. There were no counselling services in my time in my younger years in nursing, this advice and support came from our colleagues. Our senior nurses passed on the skills they had learned over time to my generation of nurses, and I hope that we too did the same for our junior nurses. Staff were so supportive to the patients in their sickness and grief and enabled many, many patients to recover, and those who did not recover spent a lifetime looking after them physically and psychologically. Through our lifetime we had spent as much time with patients as we did with our own families. I gained a great insight into life while working in St Brendan's, with all the different patient presentations and the reasons for admission. I gained the knowledge to know, that psychiatric problems can affect anyone, rich or poor, old or young, we just need to reach out and ask for help. I spent forty years working in psychiatry and I can honestly say that it was the most intriguing, extraordinary and interesting form of nursing, and even though we all have memories of injury, trauma and lived experiences, I don't regret any of my time in psychiatry, I hope I have helped some or many people recover or learn to manage and live with their illness.

There are histories of Grangegorman documented from the 1700s, when patients were expected to survive in squalid conditions, the level of depravity, filth and overcrowding were unbelievable. The cruelty human beings were subjected to lying on beds of straw that were changed every few days, patients in chains, beaten to quieten them, they had barely enough to eat to survive, there were no treatments only confinement.

In the 1800s, improvements were ongoing. Nurses were still expected to live with the patients, they were caretakers, and the male nurses were keepers. Their wages were appalling to the extent that nurses and keepers often ended up in the system when they retired, as they had no pension or savings they could barely live on their wages.

In the 1900s, conditions improved for nurses, keepers and patients. In the mid-1900s, education was provided for staff qualifications and to enhance patient care. Active engagement in work gave patients the opportunity to get away from the overcrowded wards. They worked on farms, workshops, and industrial therapies. New treatments were introduced, major tranquilisers, insulin therapy, malarial therapy, straight E.C.T. Many of these therapies had severe side effects and some were discontinued and replaced with safer medications, psychotherapy, modified E.C.T., counselling, cognitive behavioural therapy and child and adolescent services. The patient now has an umbrella of services and care plans that are constructed with the patient with all the various disciplines, doctors, advanced nurse practitioners, clinical specialist's nurses, auxiliary staff, psychology, occupational therapists, physiotherapy and home care teams.

Nurses, doctors, and nursing unions have worked tirelessly to enhance patient care. So many people were misplaced and admitted into psychiatric hospitals for various reasons: land deals, unmarried mothers, unresolved trauma etc. Some people spent their whole lives in institutions as they felt safer when they became institutionalized than facing the real world if they were discharged. The hospital became their asylum. Many patients had no relatives, and in some cases, if they had relatives, they wanted them out of the way in the institution because of the stigma around mental illness. Many children taken into care were in industrial schools, mother and baby homes, lost their independence and self-esteem, and were not given educational opportunities to gain employment. At eighteen when they left industrial schools and mother and baby homes where they were exploited and worked for the duration of their stay there. They had no hope of gainful employment. If people were not educated or successfully got an apprenticeship in trades, they were unable to gain employment, and some of them ended up in psychiatric hospitals around the country. In my time, nursing patients could be quite difficult to manage and dangerous if they were psychotic. You relied on your fellow nurses for training on the job, with no manual handling training, overcrowded conditions, or basic equipment. The theory was aspirational, but actually doing the job was quite different and hands-on. Education and training improved in the 70s but modern equipment was hard to access, the health boards never had any money—that's what we were told anyway.

It's comforting to know that nursing has improved somewhat for the patient, but a lot more needs to be done to avoid long waiting lists, over crowdedness, Accident and Emergency departments, early diagnosis and treatment for people with psychiatric and medical problems.

Our ministers might gain an insight into everyday nursing in hospitals and nursing homes if they visited hospitals, nursing homes and care facilities around the country. Nursing is 24/7 it's not a typical Monday to Friday job. Psychiatric patients present with the same symptoms as they did fifty years ago. It's how they are treated today and in the future that really matters. The closing down of psychiatric hospitals around the country has led to people with dementia, being admitted to general hospitals until they are placed in nursing homes or under the care of Psychiatry of Old Age service. People present with various other psychiatric conditions psychosis, depression, suicidal ideation, paranoia drug and alcohol addiction, presenting to their G.P., or in Accident and Emergency departments until they are assessed by the psychiatric team in Accident and Emergency or psychiatric clinics around the country. That person could be you or me someday, and the people who fall through the cracks often end up homeless, in prison, and untreated for their illness.

My Life and My Experience of Working in Psychiatry

I had just finished my leaving certificate and like most seventeen-year-olds, hadn't made my mind up as to what I wanted to work at. I was offered a job as a temporary teacher in the local, national school while a teacher was on maternity leave in September, so I said I might as well give it a try.

I had been working for the summer looking after my friends' children in the town. I had a lovely summer. I had a boyfriend, and on his day off, he used to bring me and the two boys I was minding for drives in the country or the beach. When I started teaching in September, one of the little boys I babysat was in my class. He was used to calling me Lucy. I told him when he was in class, he had to call me teacher. Every other summer, I had worked on our fruit farm at home and babysat a couple of nights a week. At Christmas, I was informed that the teacher would be returning in January, so that was the end of my teaching, though I really enjoyed it.

Then I saw an ad for a teaching job in Skerries, Co Dublin. I applied and had an interview with the canon in the priest's house. The interview was very informal , he just asked me how

I did in my leaving cert, and that was that, he asked me if I could start next week, he told me to go to a house near the Home Patrick Hotel where two teachers lived, and I might get accommodation. I called to the house, met the teachers, explained the situation, and they said I could share a room. I got the train home to Drogheda and then a bus to Ardee.

So I worked there from January to June, going home every Friday until Sunday night or sometimes an early train on Monday morning. My boyfriend and I would go out at weekends. This was a temporary position and I felt I should look for a permanent job as most people did at that time. I really did enjoy teaching and got lovely letters from the parents of many children asking me to stay, as their children had made great strides in their schoolwork and games. I was allowed to bring them to the football pitch every Friday evening for sport. I had a deal with them: if they were good all week, we would have sport every Friday afternoon. It was tough, I had three classes in one room, baby infants, high infants and first class, so I had a lot of juggling to do to see to each class. My cousin Pat worked in Grangegorman and used to visit us in Ardee regularly. Pat said they were always looking for staff in Grangegorman, so I applied and got a date for my interview on 25th August 1972.

I had arrived, my dad had just dropped me off for my interview. I had applied for a job as a psychiatric nurse at Grangegorman Psychiatric Hospital. I did not want to work in the psychiatric hospital in Ardee as my dad worked there, and I would always be known as "Dick Mc Guinness's daughter."

As an eighteen-year-old from the country, I found it quite daunting when I arrived in Grangegorman. The big, iron black entrance gates were like they would lead into a prison, but I thought they were beautiful and secure for the people inside the walls. These gates of the hospital were on the right-hand side of the road and all the buildings were grey granite, they looked stunning. The hospital my father worked in, in Ardee, was red brick, as were many hospitals around the country. I asked a nurse in uniform where the nurses' home was. She told me that it was on the opposite side of the road. The nurses' home also had big iron black gates that were opened, this was the appointed place for my interview.

The nurses' home was a large building with four floors, black iron gates and railings to the front, and was built in a square, the lower part in grey granite, and the rest of the building in red brick. The big wooden entrance door, with a coat of arms over the door, was open that day. It would normally be locked, with a pass key, a large key that every nurse had. I went in and was greeted by the sister in the nurses' home. This nurse looked after the running of the home and its occupants, nurses and their rooms, doctors on call, and doctors' quarters, sick bay, nurses' sitting room for their breaks, and nursing administration offices.

I was escorted into a side room known as the sacred heart room until I was called for the interview. There were three other girls there also from the country. I was called in second and sat before a panel of three people: the Matron, the Head male nurse and a Hospital administrator. They asked informal questions about where you were from, how you got on in your leaving cert, and most of all, why you wanted to be a nurse. Naturally, I said I wanted to look after people and help them if I could and wanted to be a nurse. The interview lasted about fifteen minutes.

I was asked to wait outside in the sacred heart room. The

interviews were finished, and we were all asked if we could start on next Monday the 29th of August. This was Thursday. We did not have much time to decide. We all said yes and we were all very excited of not alone working in the largest psychiatric hospital in the country but moving to Dublin from small towns around the country. The third building is the new building replacing the original nurses' home, front and back.

Old nurses' home front view as it was then.

The back of the old nurses' home.

New building replacing the old nurses' home with the same gates.

My dad collected me at the gates that evening at 5 p.m., he had union business. He was a nurses' representative in the ILTGWU (The Irish Transport and General Workers Union) in Liberty Hall. There were no direct busses from the hospital, so I was glad of the lift. It was the only way I could get home. I had only been to Dublin City once or twice before on school excursions. I had spent the rest of that day looking around the buildings. The place seemed huge with buildings on both sides of the road. The hospital stood on eighty-five acres of land, which was quite extensive in this part of the city. My dad pulled up in the van. We didn't have a car as we were a large family of twelve children. "Well," he said, "did you get it?"

"Yes," I said happily. He was a psychiatric nurse for many years and worked all of his life in the local psychiatric hospital in Ardee Co Louth. I had decided to apply for Dublin as I wanted something exciting. I had just broken up with my boyfriend, who I was in love with at that time, but it was over, and I needed a fresh start, to meet new friends and explore new places.

At the weekend I started packing a few things together, and I said my goodbyes to my friends. We were informed we would be getting a couple of uniforms for duty so we would only need our casual wear for our time off. Monday morning, Dad gave me a lift to the hospital, he was probably glad I got fixed up with a permanent and pensionable job. My sister also started nursing at Monaghan Psychiatric Hospital the week before. He must have thought, *great another two off the list, there were still six siblings living at home.* I said goodbye, and that was goodbye to living at home except for holiday visits.

We made our way up the grounds to the school of nursing where we were to have two weeks in block, which meant two weeks of tuition with no nursing duties, prior to this people got off the wards for classes and were expected to study and work at the same time. This new system allowed nurses to study for four two week periods at specified times throughout the year without nursing duties, the rest of our nursing experience was learned by working on the wards, "hands-on" we learned the practical and the theory to get our qualification.

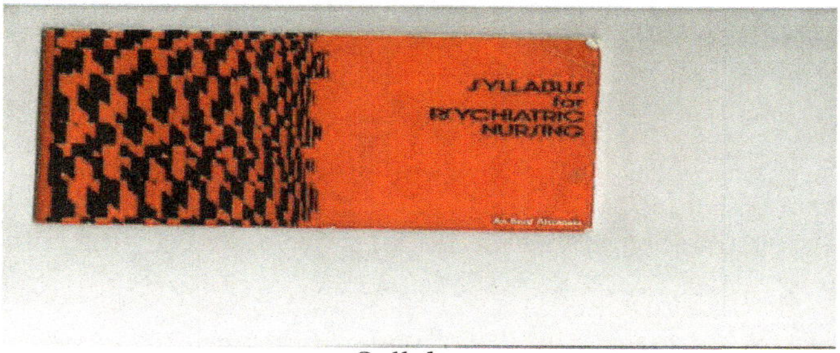

Syllabus

I was surprised to see many more nurses starting that day, eighty in total, two classes of forty, twenty males and twenty females in each. We were introduced to our tutors, a solemn-looking lady who was head of the school of nursing and two other tutors who would cover the syllabus between them. It was very exciting seeing all the new faces, and throughout those two weeks, we got to know each other. The majority of people were from the country with only a few nurses from Dublin. We were given our syllabus book which we had to keep until we were qualified, which was signed by the charge nurse on each of the wards we were assigned to. This little book recorded the skills we were learning throughout our training.

We were given a brief tour of the hospital and grounds, the hospital was divided into two parts, the upper part on the right-hand side of the road which consisted of several units.

Front gates of the hospital and the upper house.

Inside the big gates on the left, there was a building they called the block, which was a high-security unit with five units: O, P, Q, R, and the NFA (no fixed abode) unit, then further to the left of that were Units 23 and 23A, and the Operant Unit. The units in the block had an enclosed exercise space for these patients so they could have some space outside. There were two churches, one Catholic between 23 and 23A and the protestant church opposite the Catholic Church, which was near a tunnel under Grangegorman road which joined the two parts of the hospital, the upper house and the lower house. The Catholic Church known as St Laurence's Chapel, was built in 1850, and the church of Ireland-protestant church was built in 1860.

To the right of the gates was the morgue, now refurbished and further up that path were the admission units 3A, 3B, 10A and 10B, towards the front of the hospital was the Assessment unit. On we went further up the grounds where next was the Pharmacy, and The Occupational Therapy Department. Next, there were more two storey units 2, 4, 6, 7, and 8. Behind these

Catholic Church St Brendan's.

Protestant Church

units was the front hall another beautiful building and an infirmary, Unit 5, for very physically ill patients where operations would have been performed by outside consultants before my time. On the right were units 1A, 1B, 1C, and Unit 9, a large kitchen where meals were prepared for these patients, and a dining room where the patients from these units would have their dinner each day. On the left, opposite these units, there was the school of nursing on the top floor and a recreational hall on the ground floor. The school of nursing was where we were to attend our lectures. During our training, the school was also used for in-service training for staff for refresher courses, various workshops and presentations.

The morgue refurbished as it is now.

Front Hall

There was a carpenter's workshop and a general room which could be used for the male nurses, male attendants, and male household staff to have tea breaks etc., as the female nurses, nurses' aids, and household staff had a large sitting room in the nurses' home, which was totally out of bounds for the male nurses, attendants, and household staff. Further on from these units, there were large playing pitches, a ball alley and a hut for people, the lads mostly, to shower and change, a very primitive communal one when playing matches. I can only remember using this building once or twice when we were playing mixed matches.

The pitches also included a ball alley and a very well-kept bowls pitch. The football and hurling pitches extended right down to the churches, where there was a hockey pitch, the bowls team were involved in many events and matches before my time. I thought to myself, this place was very large and this was just the upper house, you would need a map to get around.

The changing hut before and after matches, with a very primitive cold shower.

A group of male nurses attending a wedding outside a church.

The old staff canteen the small building.

We were sent to lunch to the old canteen, now the derelict building to the right, which was in the lower house on the left side of the road behind the nurses' home. We had a lovely lunch, actually dinner, and met back at the nurses' home for the second part of the tour of the lower house. The staff in the canteen were always very pleasant and used to serve the meals, years afterwards it became self-service and the canteen was moved to the upper house. The Lower house consisted of eleven units which were built in a square, and also included a laundry, a therapy unit, and a shop, a large kitchen with chefs and assistants to cater for the meals for the patients in the lower house, approx. 500, including L, M and N, three units near the Broadstone, and further on there was a boiler house and a tinsmiths shop, all having their own staff for the different qualifications and skills.

There was a canteen for the patients, and a little shop, where any able-bodied patient who might have a few bob from working in the adjoining therapy could buy little treats for themselves. The therapy had activities like sewing, knitting, and art materials. Some patients used to repair nightshirts and nightdresses for the patients. Some of the ladies in my first unit were able to attend therapy Monday to Friday, and some patients operated the little shop. When I went to the front of this building, which was best viewed from the pathway to the Richmond Hospital, I thought it looked stunning with a coat of arms over the entrance. To the right of this building was an iron gate with access by our pass key that led to the Morning Star Hostel for the homeless. This gate was very handy for us if you were on duty in the lower house as you could get into town very quickly walking.

Lower house

The front of the lower house with the coat of arms at the entrance.

There were also three units, L, M, and N, a three-storey building near the Broadstone bus station, which housed long-stay patients with varying disorders, approximately 120, with forty patients in each unit. All of these patients were female, with a variety of different diagnoses. Some had checkered histories and could be very paranoid and dangerous.

The annexe, a beautiful architectural building was next to the nurses' home. The famous clock tower still stands over the annexe, the date inscribed on the weathervane is 1816. The Annexe was formerly a women's prison in 1812, which closed in 1826 and was subsequently handed over to the hospital. Before it was a prison it operated as a fever hospital during an outbreak of typhus in 1818, and in 1832, it was used as a cholera hospital that claimed the lives of 4,478 Dubliners between March and December of that year. It was so highly contagious, it killed victims within twelve hours of contraction.

This annexe was used for administration purposes with many different departments, the typing pool, even a credit union office for the staff, and the administrator's office for looking after everyone's interests, various accounts, patient accounts, and administration documentation in the hospital. This building also held old records of patients who had died in the hospital, these records were stored on the top floor of the annexe, but access was out of bounds. The building to the left side of the annexe, with its own gate, was the stores department, which also had its own staff, where all food, clothes, linen, towels all sorts of equipment that were needed on a daily basis for the patients in the hospital. The store's department also operated as a welfare store where people on welfare arrived in vans and loaded up their goods free of charge: beds, cots chairs, mattresses, buggies, all sorts of equipment. This always amazed me, especially when I would be saving to buy a buggy for my kids. Our tour was finished and I would need another map to get around the lower house.

There were approximately I, 600 patients in the hospital when I started in August 1972. The nurses' home which was built in 1949, where the first-year students were allocated a room, at least for the first year, unless you were from Dublin, as you could live at home. The nurses home at that time was for female nurses only, no male nurses were ever allowed inside except to the sacred heart room to collect you for a date, so you had to kiss or cuddle your loved one at the gates of the nurses home, or at the side of the annexe, or if you were lucky you might fall for someone who had a flat.

There were restrictions in the male nurses' residences too, even though they were not policed like the nurses' home. I did hear one time some male nurse was sacked for having a female nurse in the residence. Many years later, in 1999 when the recruitment of nurses was very low, they actually accommodated male and female nurses in the home, what luxury and freedom the younger nurses had twenty-five years later, all living in the nurses' home. I can only imagine what Matron Glennon would say about that, it would not even be contemplated in our day.

The Annexe.

I was very interested in when this hospital was built and its history. I discovered the history of St Brendan's from various sources. The History of Grangegorman by J. Reynolds 1992, Music and Madness by Ivor Browne 2008, Gateway magazines 1968 to 1974. This magazine was printed in the occupational therapy department by PJ Reynolds, Jackie Ledwidge, and other staff, and patients and staff were invited to submit letters or articles every month. There was lots of news in the magazine as to who was getting married, going to England to do their general training, who was having babies, and a sports section from St Brendan's and St Ita's. Some of the patients would submit poems, which were excellent.

St Brendan's dates back to the 14th century when Grangegorman was the location of a splendid manorial residence, a small village had grown up in the northern quarter known now as Manor Street. The whole site of Grangegorman was given to Francis Adgard in the mid-16th century for services to the crown. The manor had several owners after that. One of the owners, Sir John Stanley who spent most of his time in England with his principal correspondent, Dean Swift who proposed the building of an asylum for the poor and the insane people of Dublin. In 1773 the house of industry was opened by the corporation for the relief of the poor in the city of Dublin. This house soon found offering refuge to the less violent type of mad persons or lunatics as patients were referred to, while the uncontrollable human beings/lunatics, were sent to an old building called the St James Street Bridewell, and on the recommendation of the physician to the house of industry, these "Lunatics" were chained in stalls, their diet was stirabout and buttermilk. Over time, the house attracted the insane from all parts of the country which evidently led to such overcrowding the governors asked the commons for more buildings. In 1810, the first instalment for the building of the new Richmond Asylum, 12,000 pounds was granted, with Francis Johnson acting as an architect who based the plans on our Lady of Bethlehem Hospital London, which we knew as the Lower house. In 1814, the Richmond Asylum had its first admission. In 1815, it had a board of fifteen governors, two physicians, Alexander Jackson and Hugh

Ferguson and a surgeon, Andrew Johnson. The moral governor as head of the asylum and answered to the board of governors.

The institution was controlled in 1814 by the Governors of the House of Industry.

In 1815 an act of parliament appointed separate asylum governors. The first of the moral governors was Richard Grace from 1815 to 1830, followed by Dr William Heisse for only ten months, then by Samuel Wrigley from 1831 to 1857, the asylum was known as "Wrigley's asylum."

Then medical superintends were appointed:

- Dr Joseph Lawlor (1857-86)
- Dr Connolly Norman (1886-1908).
- Dr John O'Connor (1908-37).
- Dr John Dunne (1937-66.)
- Professor Ivor Browne (1966 onwards).

In 1930, the institution was called the Richmond District Asylum, the first mass was celebrated in 1936, and the Catholic and Protestant churches were built. In 1850, the hospital acquired further lands and in 1895, a residence was built for the Resident Medical Superintendent on the north circular road called "St Dymphna's," which subsequently was used for an alcoholic unit. In 1894, lands were acquired in Portrane Co. In Dublin, where St Ita's Hospital was built, a farm was developed there, which supplied St Brendan's and St Ita's with fresh fruit, vegetables and pork.

In the early years of the Richmond Asylum the governors insisted that the nurses be locked in with their charges, the wages were very poor. In 1840 a female nurse's wages were £6.6s annually, this was equivalent to four old pence the price of a gentleman's newspaper. Male keepers as the male nurses were called were paid £11.00 annually, and carpenters were paid £13.2s, much more than any nurse. Nurses and keepers were provided with clothing/uniforms. Gratuities of one guinea was paid annually to staff for good behaviour.

The Registered Medical Superintendent was paid £305 annually, given a furnished house, provided with coals, candles and soap. He was also allowed to keep two pigs. Just imagine the life of a psychiatric nurse then. Special leave was required before leaving the grounds, these conditions were pretty stark for nurses at that time. When special leave was granted, if a nurse or keeper came back drunk, they got one warning and on a second warning were sacked.

There were ways of handling troublesome inmates, they had a Frantic Ward where they were held in solitary confinement with their arms secured, probably like a strait jacket used in our time. The benefits of modern diagnostic and therapeutic therapies were not available, the medical professions' hands were tied by the governors and the lack of empirical or theoretical knowledge was evident. Over the years, the lack of funding prevented improvements for inmates, and that situation continued during my time in psychiatry. An inspection in 1824 reported conditions as being "deplorable." The asylum being filthy, patients in badly ventilated rooms or cells, long periods of restraint were common, patients lying on straw which had to be cleaned out daily like a horse's stall, and nurses were described as ill-instructed, not quite qualified, and elderly. Although the inspection led to some improvements, the lack of funding remained.

Between 1857-85 the numbers of patients increased from 600-1,100. Dr Lawlor at that time was worried that many patients were being admitted for legal reasons. We have all heard stories of committals over land or property, and of course unmarried mothers. The overcrowding continued. In 1890 report described patients sleeping on floors, the halls, every inch of space available. The solution, for the inspectors was to build a new asylum in Portrane Co. Dublin the railway line was a big factor in this decision, and by 1902, St Ita's was built. This hospital accommodated 900 patients from St Brendan's, to relieve the overcrowding, Later in the mid-80s more patients with intellectual disability were also transferred, as St Ita's staff who trained in Intellectual Disability nursing, had the expertise in this area, as a lot of patients were inappropriately admitted to St Brendan's with this condition, which needed a very different approach to treatment, rather than a patient with a psychiatric disorder.

In the 1890s, Dr Norman arranged for formal education for nurses, he arranged lectures and demonstrations, and as a result, a state exam was set by the Medico-Psychological Association, when this exam was passed nurses were known as Psychiatric nurses. He reported that patients benefited from educated nurses and also arranged the education of junior doctors. Despite all of these improvements overcrowding was still a problem in 1898. The hospital had 2,375 patients.

Professor John Dunne was appointed as Medical Superintendent in 1937. Having studied abroad in Vienna he noticed that inoculation of malaria was effective for patients with G.P.I. (general paralysis of the insane), and on his return to Ireland, he gave malarial therapy to 150 patients with G.P.I. known as general paralysis of the insane or dementia paralytica which was once a fatal syphilitic infection and one of the major reasons for psychiatric hospitalization. Professor Dunne noticed a remarkable improvement with malarial therapy. When he was appointed to St Brendan's with 3,400 patients, he was also appointed to St Ita's the total number of patients was for both hospitals. He recalls that St Brendan's in the late 1930s was a great community of medical, nursing, and auxiliary staff. The hospital was pretty self-sufficient with workshops, operating theatres and recreational facilities. Sporting activities included cricket, tennis, football matches, dances, concerts and patient outings. The famous high stone wall which surrounded the hospital was to keep outsiders out and to protect the patients within. There were many treatments introduced. In 1938, E.C.T. (electroconvulsive therapy), major tranquilisers, and insulin coma therapy. Phenobarbitone and morphia were the most common drugs used in St Brendan's in the 1930s.

Lobotomy, involving the surgical separation of the frontal lobes of the brain, was performed on hundreds of patients in Grangegorman. This procedure according to a senior consultant was the biggest single mistake in the history of psychiatry. This practise of performing lobotomy was worldwide leaving the patient docile and easy to manage, but they had lost their former personality. This operation was practised worldwide. There were even rumours of Robert Kennedy's daughter having this operation in the U.S.A. The Richmond Lunatic asylum was changed to St Brendan's in 1958 with its population was 2,000 patients. The wards were grossly overcrowded where patients were herded into large dayrooms during the day and sleeping in overcrowded dormitories and corridors at night. There could be no therapeutic interventions or rehabilitation until this situation was resolved. Imagine the difficulties nurses and auxiliary staff faced trying to ensure everyone got enough to eat, and even discover a patient with physical ailments, and notice changes in their mental state.

Dr Dunne had made several submissions to the minister and the board regarding overcrowding stating the one ward alone contained 160 patients instead of eighty which even then seemed impossible. While government ministers were advocating for advances in modern psychiatry they were ignorant of the supports in the community and the finances that would be needed to make these changes.

Some improvements were made regarding overcrowding in 1957. The former tuberculosis sanatorium Crooksling in the foothills of the Dublin Mountains was acquired by the hospital, where 200 female patients were transferred there. These TB hospitals were built on the commitment and dedication of Dr Noel Browne in 1948, where isolation and fresh air was the only treatment available, until a pharmaceutical company Merk, developed an antibiotic for the treatment of TB.

Dr Noel Browne was the minister for health from 1948-1951. He was passionate in his attempts to eradicate T.B as his mother, father, and sister had died from T.B, not to mention 10,000 children a year, he believed in health for all whether you were rich or poor. He tried to introduce the mother and baby free medical care, but medical, political and religious opposition to the scheme, and the fact that it was shot down by the first inter party government of Taoiseach John Costello in 1951. This remains the greatest political controversy in modern Irish history. He resigned as minister for health. He found it hard to find work, and trained in Psychiatry, he worked in St Brendan's in the early sixties for a few years before returning to politics where he tried to introduce legislation for healthcare. He died in 1997.Many of my colleagues remember working with Dr Noel Browne and had the greatest respect for him.

To alleviate the overcrowding in the hospital, many patients were also transferred to St Loman's, and many geriatric patients transferred to St Mary's Hospital in the phoenix park. It took nearly half a century for improvements for patient's standard of living, and a reduction in overcrowding as advocated by Dr Connolly Norman, and Dr Dunne. Ministers and government were never depending on lunatics to vote for them for their successive governments, lunatics were seen as the dregs of society, to be hidden away, treated like slaves or worse in the first half of the 18th century. Dr Dunne had made several submissions to the minister and the board regarding overcrowding. In 1959 the government at last said the financial situation had changed and they could improve the living conditions for the patients in St Brendan's, some of the older temporary buildings were replaced by new ones. The new admission units 3A and 3B with forty females upstairs and thirty males downstairs, an assessment unit, an outpatient department and teaching unit for junior doctors and the lecture theatre. Admission units 3A, 3B, on the right, assessment unit, OPD and lecture theatre on the left.

Conditions for nurses improved, from 1945 onwards, in 1948 a nurse tutor was appointed in St Brendan's, and a similar post in St Ita's in 1949, nurses were not expected to do non nursing duties, like working in kitchens, gardening, domestic work, or wardsportering, van driving, working in the stores department etc. These changes took a long time to come into effect as Dr Dunne concluded that working in all these areas was therapeutic for patients, and they should be supervised by nurses, who would be very perceptive to mood changes, calming down volatile situations, and de-escalating violent incidents. So in my time starting in 1972, there were nurses in charge of running the occupational therapy, the laundry anywhere patients were occupied. This practise worked well, and the main benefit was for patients to be actively engaged in some form of work, time spent out of the wards, they were all paid a small fee for this work.

Assessment unit: 3A and 3B

Prior to 1945, all patients were either voluntary or temporary (involuntary) signed in by a relative or others in authority, or persons of unsound mind (P.U.M.). After the 1945 Mental Treatment Act, we saw the introduction of more voluntary patients, who were admitted of their own accord, but there was still a need for involuntary or temporary patients, as there still is today.

In 1966, Professor Ivor Browne became R.M.S. of St Brendan's. He, like his comrades before him, had studied abroad and gained experience in London, Harvard, and Boston and made several trips to India and the Greek islands of leros.

He began to reorganize the hospital into catchment areas and dividing the hospital into three community psychiatric teams, team 1-James Connolly Memorial Hospital, team 2-Vergemount at Clonskeagh and team 3-St Vincent's Fairview. Then he began reorganizing the units within St Brendan's Hospital, categorizing the patients by age and psychiatric disability. This categorization of patients was not very successful as old and young were all admitted to the admission units, some older people were transferred to the lower house if a vacancy occurred when someone passed away.

Dr Browne set up the assessment unit where patients would present for admission unless they were brought in by police escort and needed admission to the secure units. I was on duty one night in the assessment unit when the guards arrived with a very disturbed lady in handcuffs, they wanted to bring her into the assessment unit, but I knew her and her history. She would cause havoc if we let her in, so the doctor on duty and I, sensibly got into the Garda van as we knew she would need to go to the secure unit directly, so the guards asked us to escort them in the van with her, which we did, and we brought her into the unit. The doctor was following me, I told the Gardaí they could take off the cuffs and go, as soon as we were inside the unit, as the staff knew her well.

The assessment unit gave some time to assess people for the most appropriate unit that they should be admitted to, sometimes patients might spend a night or two there and were discharged without admission, this practise gave the wards some time to prepare to accept the patient during daylight hours, as prior to this, patients were admitted to wards at all hours day and night, which in turn was very distressing for the resident patients in each unit at night.

The assessment unit also held large outpatient clinics for patients' psychiatric review, bloods, and for depot clinics (patients on long-term injections) who were not agreeable to taking regular medication, but would come for their injection every two weeks or monthly depending on their diagnosis. I took part in the operation of these clinics with the doctors and nurses. Some days we would give up to forty or fifty injections, take bloods and organize patients to see the doctors in turn for review. One senior doctor was of Indian origin, we didn't even need to ask if he had arrived for the clinic, the waft of garlic and spices would immediately let you know he was there.

Dr Ivor Browne secured a number of beds in private hospitals, such as St Patrick's Hospital and St John of Gods Stillorgan for public patients. These arrangements were in place when I started as a student nurse in 1972. I worked in St Brendan's with Professor Ivor Browne as RMS, I always found him very approachable. He always carried his tin whistle in his inside pocket. We would have weekly meetings in the assessment unit when I worked in 3B, and in the middle of a meeting if there were disagreements, he would often excuse himself for five minutes, go outside and play his tin whistle, then the meeting would resume on his return. He obviously found this as a way of calming things down for himself, as he often admitted to us.

We were not allowed into the wards until we were assigned to a ward in due course. We were measured up for our uniforms size wise, just the females, the lads just had to wear white coats over their clothes. Our uniform consisted of a striped heavy cotton navy and a white dress resembling a nightshirt, starched white aprons, and a clip-on collar, white pull-up cuffs up to our elbows and a starched white hat and a belt.

Nurses in uniform outside the nurses' home. The final class of 1968.

Matron, Miss Glennon and Sister Tutor, Miss O'Neill.

Professor Ivor Brown, Chief Psychiatrist.

We were also given a female pass key which opened all of the doors in the female wards, my key was number 438. The male students were given a male pass key for the male wards, these keys were made in Wolverhampton, I presumed that this was a security reason as they were imported and were hard to come by. There was no mixing of staff in the wards until a later date; the only exception was the infirmary and the assessment unit. We were warned that if we lost the key it would cost us five pounds, nearly a week's wages, we were assigned a room and given our key my room was 162 on the fourth floor, I liked my room as it was to the front of the nurses home and I could look out onto the road at night, other rooms were at the side or the back of the building and were darker.

In our rooms we had a bed, a built in wardrobe and a sink, a small locker by the bed and central heating they were quite cosy, and anything else you wanted you had to buy yourself. We got a kettle, mugs etc., to make our tea at night. There were four bathrooms on each floor. The baths were rusty in parts but you had to just ignore that if you wanted a bath, some of us got a hose attachment, and used the bath as a makeshift shower, and toilets were scarce enough, with two at each side of the building four on each floor, not very many for so many nurses. You had to take your chance as to when a bathroom might be free.

I suppose we were lucky to get a room as prior to this some nurses had to sleep in rooms of the patients wards. The fourth floor had the advantage of easy access to the roof, we would go up there on our days off if it was sunny and we had a great view over the whole area. The only disadvantage to my room was it was opposite one of the deputy matron's rooms, so we had to be quiet if I had any of the girls calling. It took a while getting into the uniform in the mornings, so getting up earlier was a must, it took at least fifteen minutes, our uniforms were washed and starched in the hospital laundry, or a lot of time would be wasted washing and starching, which probably would not have met with the standard of dress that was expected. We started each day at 7 a.m. and finished at 8:30 p.m. I wondered how long I would last in this profession, but it was early days, too soon to imagine.

I met my future husband, which I didn't know then, in the dining room. This was after working a few weeks in the hospital. He was having lunch with his friend John and we sat at the same table. He asked me out, he was of course a sportsman, handsome, nice, warm temperament, lean figure, a glint in his eye, and a few years older than me, he was two years qualified, I accepted and we went out during the week, just a regular date which I enjoyed and we said goodnight at the nurses home with a passionate kiss.

I had a few brief encounters with some other nice guys the first few weeks when we started, but I knew they were just flings, we were all testing the waters at that time. It must have been love at first sight for my now husband, as he asked me to marry him three weeks later. I was flabbergasted and said, "Ask me again in a year's time when we got to know each other." While we had the chemistry, I wanted to get my qualification and somewhere to live, a house, not a flat, before taking the plunge of marriage that would be a few years down the road. I knew he was the right one for me but he needed to prove it, and it was very early days. I had seen too many people renting in Dublin, the rents were quite expensive and rooms for rent were usually in the form of bedsits with a bed room cum kitchen in the corner of the room, a kettle, a two ringed cooker, few presses, and a shared bathroom on a landing which you had to book, imagine, you would never get your forever home if we went down that road. So we continued seeing each other for four years, before getting married.

My first assignment was to the lower house. This building was built in a square with units B, C, D, E, F, G, H, I, J, and K, the kitchen/catering department, canteen for patients, and tinsmith shop. The building was three stories high in the shape of a square, with an enclosed outdoor area with seating where patients were allowed access to for recreational purposes which the units on the ground floor opened out onto.

This building had no lifts, so access to the units was by large stone steps of stairs. Underneath this building, there were shelters for patients during the war. My first assignment was to unit E, on the ground floor. I remember opening the entrance door with my pass key and reporting for duty. I noticed the smell of urine just when I went in but after a while you just didn't notice. There were thirty-two female patients in this unit, most of them needing full nursing care, there were a group of six ladies who slept in a side dormitory, and the remainder slept in a large dormitory which was the custom at that time.

There was no time for slacking in this unit as the staffing assigned was the charge nurse, and two staff nurses on a good day, myself (student) and another student and a domestic, the person who looked after the kitchen, collecting the meals from the main kitchen on a trolley, serving out the meals, cleaning etc., we also had to help with non-nursing duties, as in cleaning patients lockers, bed tables and laundry which all had to be counted, dirty going out, and clean laundry coming in, with different bags for each items. The laundry was marked in permanent black marker with each unit on each item. Time seemed to go so fast, with an hour for dinner and tea, technically it was supposed to be three quarters for dinner, and a half hour for tea, with a ten-minute morning and afternoon tea break, you worked one day, off the next, it was known as day on day off, the shift was long from 7:15 a.m. until 8:30 p.m., it was later changed from 8 a.m. to 8:30 p.m.

These patients needed round-the-clock care. They had to be fed, washed, dressed, mobilized, occupied if possible, and above all talked to. Many of these patients had no relatives, and some relatives had visited often or very seldom, and some patients had no one at all. So the nurses were very important to these patients and were often the only friends they had. When a person died that old saying came into play, where there's a will, there's a relative, this happened several times, just when you would think a person had no one belonging to them until they died, then they all appeared out of the woodwork, there was such a taboo about relatives being in Grangegorman, or the mad house as it was often referred to.

Many of these patients were now in a physically rigid state, unable to bend their arms and legs. In later years there was a suggestion that the medication to treat psychiatric illness may have caused damaging side effects like these. These old ladies took a lot of energy to wash, dress, and feed because of their rigid physical state, they would pull against you, as sometimes they were uncooperative in keeping them clean, hydrated, and well nourished. Some of these patients needed cot sides to prevent them from rolling or falling out of the bed, these cot sides were heavy steel cot sides, we would take them off, make up the bed and then put them on again.

Occasionally if a patient had to go to a general hospital usually the Richmond, or the Mater, they would invariably come back to us with a bed sore. We would immediately start the healing process with diligence, cleaning the wound, dressing it, using bed cradles to keep the weight of the blankets of any wound until it healed. If patients were chesty, we had back rests, again had to be mechanically positioned to sit the patient up to assist their breathing. There was no training in lifting techniques or any health and safety training. When I see the modern beds now with remote controls and cot sides attached to the beds, just lower down and up. I think, it's no wonder all our backs were injured using the very basic equipment we had.

We had other tasks to complete every night before going off duty, the cutlery had to be counted, God forbid if any old granny had a knife hidden and might do themselves any harm, the laundry had to be counted, God knows if there was a knickers missing or a towel, we would have to contact the laundry next day to retrieve the missing items, they would be marked with a permanent marker with the unit name which we had to check, a few patients had some of their own clothes which relatives would supply from time to time, but not very many had this luxury. I liked the homeliness and care given to these patients at night time around 7 p.m. they were all given complan, and for those able-bodied patients, they got a little drop of brandy in theirs, it was how you would treat your own granny at home. The patients on the male units would get a bottle or two of Guinness for their little nightcap, it made life somewhat comforting for them like something they would have if they lived at home.

I spent six weeks in this unit on day duty, then rostered to another unit in the Lower house, unit C, this unit was a bit different. I was amazed that some of the patients were quite independent, and slept inside rooms on a corridor. One such lady used to collect nettles every evening and was allowed into the kitchen to make nettle tea, and sometimes she made nettle soup. It's amazing to think that nettle tea is a modern product sold worldwide, how wise she was, she was in her nineties and still very healthy. Another lady was excellent at crochet and would make beautiful table mats, shawls etc. The first few months passed, it was Christmas and all of the students were rostered for night duty over Christmas and the New Year, just one of the joys of being a student, we had to grin and bear it. We had a week off after Christmas, or depending on the roster we might have had to work both Christmas and the New Year. Night duty at the time was two weeks on, and one week off, it was very tiring, it took until the middle of your week off for your body clock to adjust again.

I was assigned to Unit C on night duty. This unit was very near the Morning Star Hostel, and often homeless men would manage to find their way into the grounds of St Brendan's. When I was on night duty with my great friend Teresa, she was a senior staff nurse who I got to know very well through the GAA club, and work, we used to play poker and twenty-five in her house in the villas every Sunday night. She was like a mother to me. I used to babysit for her when my boyfriend and I were not going out to the local, the kids loved me and always ended up sleeping in my bed as kids do. The villas were houses on the Grangegorman road where staff were allowed rent for a mere sum, this practise was introduced when the hospital was built so that in the event of a fire, there would staff nearby to assist, that was the explanation given, as there was no proper fire system in the hospital at that time.

Some wards still had water buckets, which the student had to check each day to ensure they were full of water, this now seems hilarious in the event of a fire unless it was a very small one, what would three or four buckets of water do. Getting

back to our night duty in unit C with Teresa, we had everyone changed, fed and settled for the night and just after we sat on to ring in the New Year with a cup of coffee, we heard a noise in the dormitory. I went to check with a brush in my hand, and Teresa rang Security which consisted of only one man to cover all of the units in the lower house. In the dormitory, beside an old ladies bed with cot sides, I could see the window had been lifted upwards and a leg in the window. I shouted to Teresa, she said, "Hit it," so I did hit his leg. He wasn't for stopping, so both of us lashed at him with our brushes. He was half way in now, eventually, he was groaning and retreated back out the window, and we shut the window and waited for the security man which was forty minutes later. The intruder was hobbling back to the hostel when security arrived, so literally we were left to protect ourselves and the patients.

That was the start of that New Year, we finished our cup of coffee and just got on with it. There was no such thing as debriefing at that time, just write an incident report, and the security was to call more often around the grounds, which I'm sure he did not thank us for the extra work. The second time I was on night duty in this unit, six months later, we had a lady with a rare form of eczema. She was very restless in and out of bed, and every time she walked, her skin would fall off in scales. I stayed with her most of the night. She passed away peacefully in the early hours of the morning. She asked me to pray with her which I did. I was glad she had someone with her in her last hours.

My next unit was Unit D, on the ground floor, next door to Unit E. This was a similar unit with twenty patients of mixed diagnosis. I got to know these patients very well and spent quite a lot of time in this unit. If there was a vacancy on my return from holidays, I would expect to be rostered there. We had this little lady who used to live in the Dublin mountains, she settled in but would not use a toilet, she said they never had one eventually, we persuaded her, another lady had Huntington's chorea, and she lived for her husband to take her home one night a week if she was well enough.

This lady could not really talk but we got to know what she wanted, her face would light up, and she would get so excited when she saw him coming to collect her. We all knew she was going home for her night of sex and romance, but it kept her happy for as long as she was able to go. Some nurses used to say that's all he wants her for, but I felt if that's all she had and she was happy, then let her have her night of sex at home.

It obviously did her good she would arrive back beaming from ear to ear, I would say to her, "Had you a good time?" She nodded with delight. Her life expectancy was not long at her stage of the disease and she passed away a year later. Another lady had multiple sclerosis and epilepsy, she was in a wheelchair, and she was always moody and difficult to manage. Who could blame her? She was young, and the frustration used to get to her. She would throw tables, commodes (toilet seat on wheels) sometimes her food. She threw a commode full of urine on me one day, I had to go to the nurses' home and borrow a uniform from my friend. This lady had children but rarely got to see them, I met her daughter visiting her years later.

The most unusual lady we had in this unit was a lady with cancer of the brain. The top of her head was open, we dressed and cleaned it every day, and the smell was stifling. Even wearing masks, we would always decide to do her dressings before our tea break, and once we cleaned and dressed her head the stench was gone until the next day. She did not seem to be in any pain and was oblivious to it all. I firmly believe that the medication largactil she was on in large enough doses dulled the pain. She never complained and smiled through it all. She eventually passed away peacefully after approximately six months.

Another lady in this unit had a son who was schizophrenic, he used to visit her every Friday at 4. This was the time when the long-stay patients got their "comfort money," which was 8 euros a week to buy little treats for themselves in the little shop in the lower house or in whatever unit they were located. He would arrive, and she gave him the lot, she never kept anything for herself. I think she felt it was all she could do for him. She always seemed so lonely, she must have had him out of wedlock and ended up in St. Brendan's, it was hard to get her to smile. She always seemed so anxious, she had no interest in anything, but we kept trying. We would bring her to the TV room, give her magazines anything to brighten up her day. I remember when she died, it was early on a Saturday morning. We laid her out, did her makeup and her hair, did all the necessary bodily functions and dressed her.

We phoned for the porter and were informed that there was no porter on that day, we could not leave her in the unit as it was upsetting the other patients. I said to my colleague we will have to wheel her bed to the mortuary, which meant going under the tunnel to get to the other side of the hospital. This tunnel joined the upper house and the lower house, you could drive through it or walk if you were on duty in the lower house. We set off, and it took us an hour to get her there, because we has to manoeuvre the trolley and the road surface, which had potholes and was bumpy. Then we had to get the keys from the Annexe across the road, open the mortuary which we had never been in before, and wheeled her in.

We had her covered with blankets, not that she would feel the cold but to preserve her dignity in case we met anyone on route. The mortuary was a small building, and it seemed very peaceful. We left our lady there and we said goodbye. I was rostered to this unit several times as a student and a staff nurse. The next day on duty, you would be sent to Benburb Street to register the death. This street was not exactly safe at that time, it was like a red light district at night, so you wore your coat to completely cover your uniform and kept an eye over your shoulder, and you would not know who you would meet.

Next, I was on night duty in unit G, 2nd floor, one flight up, the stairs to all these units as mentioned, were stone stairs, so if you were sent to the third floor, you would need to be fit. This picture is of the original stairs, which is shiny and new now, but the structure was exactly the same except the stone steps were just stone steps and not always clean depending on if any of the male patients on the third floor decided to have a pee or worse which sometimes happened, There were no lifts in any part of the hospital.

While on night duty in Unit G one night, there was a dreadful storm, thunder and lightning. The whole dormitory lit up, like flashing images everywhere. Luckily, the patients were fast asleep. The staff nurse who was on duty with me was terrified of lightning, she was shaking and trembling. I said to her what if we sit in the corridor, the walls are so thick we would be safe. We sat there for hours, taking turns to check the patients, only I had to take all the checks. She was too terrified to budge. We eventually went into the office and I made her a cup of tea and toast. When the night matron came on her rounds, she was worried about her little dog in her car, I offered to go with her to check on him.

This dog was like her baby, he got steak for his supper every night and she ate bread with jam on it. We got to the car and he was terrified. I had brought a blanket and she wrapped him up, she thanked me and said she would stay with him until daylight and left me to find my way back to the second floor to unit G in the pitch dark. The staff nurse was still sitting in the office. I said to her we had to check all the patients again, she came with me with a flashlight. Soon it was daylight and all was well again, the joys of being a student on night duty in Unit G.

My next unit was unit B on the ground floor, with the usual layout of a dormitory and side rooms. On the front of this unit, facing the back of the Richmond hospital, was the Richmond coat of arms. This was the main entrance to the Lower house. One day on duty, I noticed a door on the corridor that was never used, it led to the underground shelter that was used during the war. This was the only unit where I saw any door that led to the underground shelter, probably because it was near to the main entrance. One day another student and I sneaked down on our break. We went down a flight of stairs, we borrowed the night torch. There was no light getting in except for some small slits in the walls. It was very derelict and was the full length of the units built on top, we walked around as far as we could go, came to another locked door and decided it was time to go back, it was eerie. It was built underground as a shelter from the bombs in the Second World War. I never heard the older nurses ever say it was ever used then, but at least they all knew it was there. I subsequently was on night duty there in unit B, it was the only unit I remember that had an open fire at night, it was so cosy and warm we topped it up with firewood that was delivered regularly. I loved night duty in that unit.

There were three units over near the Broadstone bus depot L, M, N, a three storey building. I was sent there initially as a student, forty patients in each unit, all female. Some of these ladies were independent, they could dress and eat themselves, and they had all different diagnoses. A lot of them would be receiving long acting antipsychotic injections which were administered by nurses every week, fortnight or some monthly. This was introduced as many patients were non-compliant with taking oral medication. Indeed most of them would get a daily dose of oral medication as well.

I was on duty in unit L, the bottom floor when the charge nurse asked me to go to the tinsmiths shop with one of the galvanized water buckets that was leaking. I saw the buckets on the wall, they were placed at the entrance of the unit, and she took down an empty one and off I went. I actually thought it was a joke but you didn't argue with the charge nurse, when I eventually found the tinsmiths shop in the lower house, I gave it to him, and sure enough, he put a galvanised patch on it. They really did keep these buckets full in case of fire. It would need to be a very small fire with only three or four buckets of water, it felt a bit like the dark ages.

I was telling a male friend at lunch and he said at least that was legitimate. He said he was sent to a female ward to get a pair of fallopian tubes by the charge nurse. He was so embarrassed when the ladies in the ward all had a great laugh at him. Jokes were part of the culture. When you got your exams, or if you were leaving, or going to do your general nursing, you might get a cold bath, just thrown in your uniform, shoes, and all. I had heard of this and wore a swimsuit for days under my uniform for that inevitable day, when I got my exams.

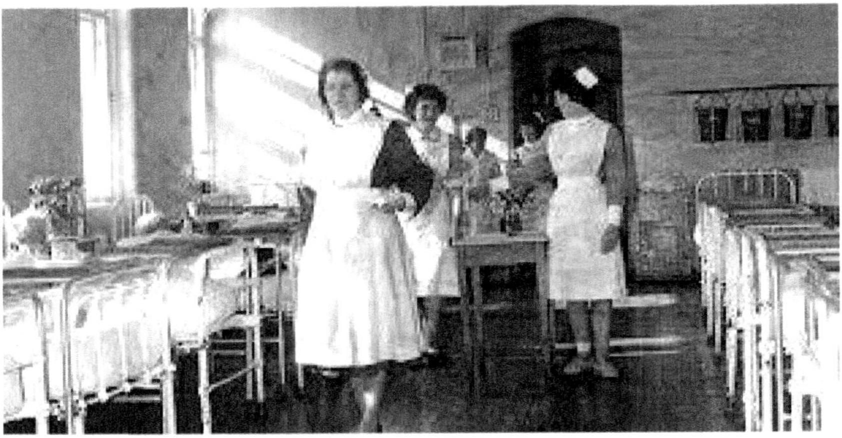

Dormitory

This picture shows what the wards looked like: wooden floors and beds very tightly arranged together, bed tables over the beds for patients who were bedridden, the cot sides were stored behind the bed, water buckets on the wall. On the big radiators that went the full length of the ward, if you were cold in the evening you could sit on these pipes, and you wouldn't be long getting warm. The older nurses would advise us not to sit on the pipes or we would get piles. Some of the wards had sidewards with six to eight beds, and other wards with some single rooms along the corridors. These single rooms were for ladies who were independent and could safely sleep in their own rooms, all rooms however had a pass key lock on them, so staff could check the patients at night time.

My next unit on night duty was Unit N on the top floor, with two large dormitories with twenty patients in each. The night matron would call around 12 p.m. and 6 a.m. After everyone was settled for the night, I had my supper, then started checking the patients with my torch to see if everyone was alive and well. On my second check two hours later, I was checking a patient who had only one lung, the charge nurse made me very aware of that at the handover of the shift, well she jumped out of bed and told me that" if I came near her again she would clatter me, and to get the hell out of her sight", so I checked her without the torch watching her abdomen rising and falling so I knew she was alive. The next night in this unit, it was very stormy and I could hear a massive explosive bang coming from the dormitory. I went in and some of the roof had fallen in, thank god nobody was hurt. I got the patients out of bed, to their annoyance, swearing at me, and moved their beds to a safer spot, then phoned for help. They eventually sent a nurse from another unit for an hour or so until things were settled. The roof was repaired the next day amazingly, so all was well again for the rest of the week. It's amazing to think of the responsibility student nurses had on night duty, you were on your own with patients who could be very dangerous.

I was back on duty in this unit, Unit N, a few years later when I was pregnant with our third child, management thought it would be a safer place to work, and I was less likely to be injured. However the three flights of stairs were difficult to navigate when you were seven and a half months pregnant. One particular day in the afternoon, when the other nurse and I had given out the cigarettes and medication, we were just having our cup of tea, we heard a thud. We ran out to investigate only to find one of the ladies had jumped over the railing and fell twenty feet below. My friend was working there in Unit M and shouted up to be, help me lift her. I said, "Don't move her, you could do more damage." There was blood coming out of her ear, I said, "Just cover her and we will get an ambulance."

I was up and down the stairs carrying my bump, we sent for the priest as well. I thought I would go into labour that day with all my hurried trips up and down the stairs, but I was ok. The ambulance came and took her away, she was unconscious. The next day, the workmen were over to the ward putting a grill up to the roof in case anyone else tried to jump again. After a few weeks, she returned to St Brendan's from Blanchardstown recovered. She was sent to a secure unit on the ground floor, she had broken her ankle and her other injuries had resolved. I think she wasn't hurt so badly because when patients are on heavy doses of tranquilisers, they flop when they fall like a baby.

As a student, you might start off the day in one unit, and be transferred to another one at any time. One day I was sent to Unit F on the second floor of the lower house, this was a very large unit with forty patients. When I arrived, the ward sister said to me take these six patients and give them their bath, I didn't even know where the bathroom was. She said it's outside the door on the left before you enter the unit, so off I went with my six ladies and found the bathroom. It was quite ingenious the way it was designed six baths in a row and six cubicles for the ladies to undress and dress after their baths. I returned to the ward with them only to be given another six and another six, so I had bathed eighteen patients before lunch. I was sent to another unit in the afternoon, and of course it was bath day, so I had another ten. I can tell you I slept well that night.

We had to live in the nurses' home for the first year, which created a lot of restrictions, the nurses home was run like a convent, no males allowed, and if you had a date, he would have to wait inside the door, in the sacred heart room until you arrived. Communication was difficult there was one public phone in the entrance hall and two extensions to every floor, there were four floors, and my room was on the fourth floor. There were two lifts which were noisy so chances were, if you did get to stay out late, you had to use the stairs, it kept us fit. The home closed at 11 p.m. every night. If you had applied for a late pass until 2 a.m. once a month which wasn't really much good, as dances in town only finished at 2 a.m. and by the time we walked home and walked we did, it would be 2.40 or so, there was no way we could afford a taxi. These were the problems we had to work around, we would ask the staff nurses to let us in, they had keys, or we would have to stay out with friends.

Once we were all grounded for a month when two of the girls were caught coming in late by the deputy matron on night duty. We all felt this was excessive and unfair, a blanket decision. Everyone was punished for two people's carelessness. We had to step up our efforts again together around this, and we did. I knew several of the girls, staff nurses who lived out in a house together, they would let me stay with them, some girls just stayed out with boyfriends. The nurses' home had its restrictions but it was warm and comfortable.

The social aspect of the job was very interesting. With eighty new nurses entering the hospital year after year, there was always great speculation as to who would go with who and who would get pregnant, new relationships were scrutinized by the older staff, and many hours were spent deliberating and a keen eye watching for any developments. The fashion in the seventies was stylish but some might say revealing with miniskirts, white or black leather boots to the knee or over, revealing cropped tops, and long maxi coats to cover it all for going out. On our days off, we wore bell-bottom trousers or shorts, platform shoes or sandals, and for dinner dances halter neck or sleeveless long dresses and capes, we thought we looked quite elegant. So I suppose for the lads, the miniskirts and boots were very enticing, my boyfriend's words.

Sports and Recreation

There were plenty of clubs, and sports were the main opportunity for engagement with hurling, football, hockey, soccer, bowls and table tennis to name but a few. Dances were held in the annexe on the top floor every second Thursday after payday which was every second Wednesday. Our wages were very poor at that time, so we had to make them last for two weeks, most people were broke the second weekend and had to survive until the next Wednesday on very little, at least living in the nurses' home you were fed. We got to socialize with other students and staff nurses, and of course we had to be back in the nurses' home by eleven p.m. or we would be locked out, it was like boarding school. If we wanted to go elsewhere, we had to apply in writing for a late night pass in advance and check if it was granted, again that was strictly two a.m., or just stay out with friends.

I always loved sport, I played camogie in school, and quickly joined in any sport I could: ladies' Gaelic and soccer teams, mixed hockey teams, and table tennis. There were more opportunities for the men than the ladies on a formal basis as there were more competitions for them. The men's teams were involved in junior, intermediate, and senior leagues and championships and were very successful.

The history of St Brendan's G.A.A. Club, which was

originally known as the Richmond Asylum Hurling Club, was founded in 1920 by Jim Doyle. The name was changed in 1923 and was then known as St Dymphna's and involved players from Portrane and Grangegorman. In 1958 the name was changed to St Brendan's to coincide with the change in name of the hospital. Prominent players in the early years of the club were the Ryan's, Paddy, Mick, Tom, Bill Flanagan, and Tony Moore. Bill Flanagan won an all-Ireland junior medal with Dublin in 1924. The St Dympna's hurlers has their first major success when they won the Dublin Junior Championship in 1950. In 1952, they won the Intermediate league and Championship as well as the Corn Eireann. Grangegorman based players were Mick Forde, Tommy Brogan, and Jackie Brennan. Tommy Conroy, Barney McCabe, Joe Tyrell and Dinny Dunne. The Portrane players included Jimmy Manton, J Carney, J Rogers, and the Stanleys. Tommy Brogan and Tommy Conroy won all Ireland junior medals with Dublin in 1952.

The club continued on into the 50s and the 60s with staff members including Dinny Neville, Mick Sommers, Eddie Gilligan, Paddy Hanley, John Mc Hale, Ollie Flynn, Paddy Gahan, Paddy Kearns, Seamus Glennon, Jack Farrelly, and Eddie Cullen. I knew all of these gentlemen even though they were finished playing when I arrived at St Brendan's. They were all still very supportive of the younger players like my husband and many more and became the mentors for the next generation of footballers and hurlers.

1970 was the most successful time in the club's history when the hurlers won the Junior Championship and the League Double 1970, in 1971 they won the Intermediate League, and in 1972 the Intermediate Championship (picture

1970 junior hurling team). The hurlers continued to pursue success and won division 2 of the senior league in 1974, they were one of the top hurling teams in Dublin in the 70s. They reached the senior hurling final in 1979 when they were beaten by Crumlin after a long delay of five weeks for the replay.

Pictures of hockey and hurling teams.

1972 2nd Hurling Team

Back Row: Mick Hagan, Pat Brennan, Paul Courtney, John Fitzpatrick, Pearse Barnett, Gerry Donnelly, Frank Kearns, Jack Buckley, Ollie Flynn.
Front Row: Padraig Tiernan, Paddy Harding, P.J. O'Connell, John Brennan, Jimmy Leslie, Mel Doyle, Mick Reilly, Seamus [illegible] Mascot is John Doyle

1973 Intermediate Football Team

Back Row: John Brennan, Pat Brennan, Tom Flinn, Gerry Ryan, Mick Fitzgerald, Conor McGee, John Higgins, James Fitzgerald, Peter Storey, Pearse Barnett, John Hughes, George Hayes, [illegible] Fitzgerald (Selector).
Front Row: Tom Hagan, Eugene Griffin, Jimmy Leslie, Willie Shanley, Willie Walsh, Joe Cassidy, Sean Dowling, Mick O'Donnell, Pat Scott, Ray Kelly, Mick Griffin.

1999 Hurling Team Junior Championship

Back (L to R): V. Redden, P. Stacey, C. O'Brien, S. O'Dowd, P. Larkin, E. Boyle, A. Mullen, G. Kelly, F. O'Connor, D. Hallan, D. Casey, P. Moran, K. Hynes, A. Kelly, J. Brennan (Manager)
Front (R to L): M. Boyle, R. O'Donnell, J. Nagle, M. Jordan, V. Burke, D. Hobbins, A. Quinsey, F. Delaney, B. O'Connor.
Front: Gerry Kelly's son and two of E. Hallan's sons

1987 Hurling Team

Back Row: Jimmy Brennan, Albert Reilly, Gerry Gray, Paddy Buggy, Seamus Brennan, Ollie O'Connor, George Hayes, Sean Hayes, Leo Scallon.
Front Row: Pat Brennan, Jimmy Walsh, Willy Shanley, Charlie Palmer, Dominic Harris, Willy Walsh, Peter Jordan. Children are Shanleys, Palmers and Harris's

ST. BRENDANS, DUBLIN A TEAM

L. to R. Front Row:- Brendan Hobbins, Dominic Harris, Tom Storey, Mick Jordan, Finian Delaney, Martin Storey, Staff Ruel, Aidan Geher and Willie Walsh.

ST. PATRICKS, DUBLIN

L. to R. Front Row: - Mylie Hurley, Eamonn Kelly, Dermot Prendergast, Brian Keegan, Paddy Burke.
Back Row:- Martin Jennings, Team Manager, Padraig Keane, Pat Flynn, Martin Donegan, David Browne and Gerry Dwyre.

ST. BRIDIG'S, BALLINASLOE

L. to R.: Front Row:- John Goode, Tony Smyth, Sean Donnellan, Tony Kilkenny, Willie Ward. Back Row: - Ollie Kilkenny, John Raftery, Michael Lohan, and J.J. Broderick.

SEVEN-A-SIDE HURLING

Grangegorman Hurley Club 1944–1945

GRANGEGORMAN CRICKET CLUB
Intermediate League Winners [illegible]

Standing: A. Moore, P. Ryan, W. Ryan, M. Ryan, W. Flanagan, J. Weir. (Umpire)
Seated: G. Tinson, J. Parker, J. Bracken, (Captain), G. Beatty, L. Dunne.

1930 Grangegorman Pipeband

ST. BRENDAN,S OF YESTER YEAR

11

In 1980 they were again in the final against Faugh's, St Brendan's won by three points, my husband Willie Walshe played on that day and indeed from 1967-1989. I remember my husband was playing a match in 1980 in Parnell Park, he was jumping up for the ball and got injured. His thumb was knocked back towards his wrist out of joint, an ambulance came and whisked him off to the hospital. I had two small kids in a buggy and could hardly drive the car. I managed to get home safely, no one could tell me which hospital they took him to. I phoned Richmond and the Mater, and he was in the Mater. The doctor said they had to wait for a surgeon from James Connolly Hospital to come to the Mater and clamp his arm and whack his thumb back into place, they said it would be some time.

It was six hours, then he got home in plaster with his football kit still on. I got a phone call from the person who managed the kit not to damage the jersey, I said, "If you think he is wearing that stinking jersey all night sleeping with me no way. I'll cut it on the seam to get it off, so I did, and by the way, he is in plaster for three weeks. We had just started our holidays, so I had a crash course in driving, and drove for the two weeks of our trip around the country.

St Brendan's G.A.A. Club went into decline in the mid-eighties due to the retirement of a number of players and the decline in staff recruitment. In 1987 they won the Junior Hurling Championship, and League Double, and in 1988 won the Intermediate League; unbelievably, Willie Walshe, Willie Shanley, and Domnick Harris were getting their second set of Junior and Intermediate medals seventeen years after their first success. St Brendan's owed its success not only by the players but the men behind the scenes. In the 1950s, St Dympnas was run by Larry Byrne and Bennie Cambell,in the mid-sixties Paddy Kearns took over training the team, which paved the way for success in the seventies. Mick Forde was chairman in the seventies, he was a father figure to players and was aided in the running of the club by Mick Sommers, P.J Carthy, Mel Doyle, G Kearns, Frank Dardis, Billy Walshe, and Jimmy Leslie. Jimmy Reilly was Chairman from 1984 to 1994, assisted by Gerry Ryan, M Farrell, P Lohan JJ Fitzgerald, and Eddie Ryan.

Picture above Willie Walshe in action on the hockey pitch.

St Brendan's 3rd XI.
Leinster Junior Cup Winners 1986-87.
M. Ryan, J. Hughes, J. Gunning, J. Brosnan, D. Bradish, J. Reynolds, M. Rohan
S. Corby (capt), B. Walsh, M. Doyle, O. Foster, P.J O'Connor, S. Wiley.

Naomh Breandain
(St. Brendan's)

Dathanna: Dubh agus Buí
(Black and Yellow)

(1)
S. Ó Maoilmhuir
(C. Palmer)

(2)
T. Ó Finn
(T. Finn)

(3)
S. Ó Braonáin
(J. Brennan)

(4)
D. Ó hEarchaí
(D. Harris)

(5)
S. Ó Mathúna
(J. Mahony)

(6)
L. Mac Seanlaoich
(W. Shanley)

(7)
P. Ó Braonáin
(P. Brennan)

(8)
S. Ó hAodha
(G. Hayes)

(9)
S. Ó Dúlaing
(S. Dowling)

(10)
L. Breathnach
(W. Walsh)

(11)
P. Ó Spealáin
(F. Spellman)

(12)
M. Bairéid
(M. Barrett)

(13)
C. Ó Beirn
(K. Berney)

(14)
P. Ó Stóirí
(P. Storey)

(15)
P. Breathnach
(P. Walsh)

Fir Ionaid: (16) M. Mac Roibín (M. Robun); (17) P. Ó hEidhin (P. Hynes); (18) M. Ó Dónaill (M. O'Donnell); (19) B. Ó Conchubhair (B. O'Connor); (20) O. Mac Floinn (O. Flynn); (21) P. Ó Baoill (P. Beale).

St Brendan's has continued on with their success by winning the Mooney Cup in 2001. The club continues on to this day, but my memories are all of the 70s and 80s and all of my lunch hours I spent minding players' children with my own, including Dessie Farrell, the current Dublin manager. Sport was a way of getting to know people better, especially the opposite sex, and my first relationship was of course with a sporting person, and as in the history of the G.A.A. Club, spent over twenty years involved with the club. I also played with the ladies' football team in the intercounty matches and also the mixed hockey inter hospitals' matches, where we would meet staff from the different hospitals.

I was marking my sister Finola, in a mixed hockey match when she worked in Portrane. I was also involved in the table tennis interhospital matches, our best player arranged all our fixtures which was no easy task. We did very well in these leagues, I played my last table tennis final against St Pats when I was seven months pregnant, we won. I gave up my sport when we had our first child Mark, as I wanted to give my husband every opportunity to play all his sports, football, hurling, hockey and soccer, golf at a later stage. He loved and lived for sport he was such an athlete. Every year there was a sports day for both patients and staff in the football pitches, consisting of tug of war, three-legged races, bicycle races, seven aside football matches, races to suit any patient who could take part, staff races. There were plenty of stands with ice cream, even chips, brick a brack, the patients loved browsing around with their few shillings.

1970
Gateway
FOURTH ANNIVERSARY NUMBER

We all had the same meeting places, dances in the boardroom, the local pub, Delaney's North King Street, where we had sing songs every Sunday night after the matches. We had a few talented musicians in the hospital, and guitars and accordions were regularly taken out, especially if the lads won their matches on Sundays. Tommy's in Manor Street was another regular meeting spot, he sponsored the golf society and supported many other functions.

Mcgowan's Pub on Phibsborough Road, another regular haunt. The playing pitches, where matches were played every week, football hurling hockey, intercounty, and interhospital matches and we would meet for table tennis practise at lunch breaks.

Life was exciting even though we had very little money to live on, we made the best use of the facilities we had.

Traveling abroad on holidays and seeing the world was out of our reach. You would dream of going to Spain or Portugal but on our measly wages, it was impossible. However one of the girls got a very good deal and asked me if I would go with her to Fuengirola. I said if I could save enough I would. Eventually we went off, she wasn't one of my best buddies but sure what could happen in a week. We arrived at night and checked out the local bars, just had a few drinks and went back to our apartment. Next day on the beach, fellas started chatting us up. I wasn't too keen, I had my boyfriend at the hospital and he warned me to be wary of the greasy Spaniards, it was just a saying, they use to use gel on their hair like the English, Irish, and other lads from other countries.

This guy asked us if we would go to a night club that night, my friend was keen, so we said we would make our own way. We got a taxi and arrived at the night club and sure enough the lads were there. One guy asked me to dance, so I did and said thanks at the end of the dance. However every time I would dance with someone else he would stand beside me. I said to my friend this guy is weird, he thinks he owns me. I had to get out of there without him knowing. The plan was I would go to the ladies, get a taxi outside and she would follow straight after me. We managed to get away and home safely. That guy was from Morocco, so I said to her no more night clubs for me I was staying local.

I was very wary of meeting him on the beach next day so we went to a different part of the beach. The next night we met three guys from Dublin who asked to join us, it felt normal, she went off with one of them but I said leave me home first. The week flew by, I enjoyed the sun, sea and sand, but I would not be rushing back. I left one asylum for a break not to be stalked by what I recognised as an unstable paranoid person. My boyfriend met me at the airport I was delighted to see him.

Back off my holidays and I was assigned to Unit R. I didn't relish going there, we heard so many stories about seclusion where people were locked in a single room or padded cell for their own safety and the safety of others when they became very disturbed and were unmanageable on the ward. They would be monitored regularly to ensure they did not harm themselves. At that time, we did not have cameras to monitor them, so we would physically go into the room in twos or threes, depending on the patients' behaviour, to take their observations, give them something to eat, or give them a toilet bowl, which often was the first thing the disturbed patient might throw at you, so we used to gently open the door to avoid the contents of the toilet bowl.

It seems very primitive now, but things have changed a lot. The secure rooms are on suite now and have monitored alarms monitored from the nurses' office, but the patient's behavior when they are psychotic is still the same, and nurses still get injured. I was on day duty in Unit R for a few weeks before my night duty. One day this old lady was admitted, she had an old coat on her and her clothes were in rags. I was asked to bathe her with another student, she was terrified, and we gently persuaded her. We put on aprons and gloves, just to get her clothes off was a struggle. We were putting her clothes into bags for fumigation, she kept holding onto her long coat, I told her we will just leave it here for you until you are washed. She agreed but kept her eye on it. She was covered in fleas we used all the lotions at our disposal to clean her.

At last the job was done, I persuaded her to go to bed, and she fell asleep. The coat was puzzling me, it was only an old filthy coat. I looked at the inside of the lining and there it was, her secret. There were bundles of money rolled up in little plastic bags and sewn into the lining. I got the other nurse to check it with me, it was nearly a thousand pounds. A lot of money at that time. We counted it with the charge nurse and sent it to the accounts office in the annexe. When she woke, she was shouting for her coat, I told her, "Your money is safe. You can get it whenever you want it when you are feeling better." She settled and was warm and safe. She got better after a few weeks of treatment, she had stopped taking her medication at home and relapsed. She was discharged and promised to keep her appointments, her relative opened a bank account with her.

I was on night duty in Unit R, for Christmas and the New Year, after spending a few weeks on day duty there. In the observation ward where we sat at night among the patients, again there was a fireplace and often at night, mice would appear. There was central heating in this unit as it was the upper house. I went to the kitchen to make the tea for the nurses' break when all the patients were settled, and when I came back in with the tray, the staff nurse was standing on the table. I asked her what was wrong and what was she doing up there, she was frozen. She pointed to the floor where two mice were running around. "I'll get the brush," I said, so I got the brush and hushed them into the fireplace and they disappeared. "You're safe," I said, she told me she was terrified of mice.

I knew the dance was on in the annexe that night. It was on New Year's Eve, we could faintly hear the music and see across the road to the annexe. I knew my boyfriend would be there, so did the charge nurse who was engaged. Before 12 midnight, she called me and told me to go over and ring in the New Year with my boyfriend. I was so delighted, so grateful to her, "I won't be long," I said.

"Take your time," she said they are all quiet now, well asleep. We rang in the New Year together, and he walked me back to the unit. At the end of that night duty I was just getting ready to go home and had left my new coat on a chair. When the day staff came on duty I still could not find my coat, and one of the ladies who had gone to the toilet was missing. So I had to walk up the north circular road in my uniform. I phoned the ward in the afternoon when I woke up to see if the patient was found. She was, but not my coat. It was my Christmas coat I had saved for, a lovely plum-coloured full-length coat, never saw it again, such is life.

I loved hearing stories from the older nurses, they were very wise, and they told us about the treatments that were used in the past, like insulin therapy for patients who were very elated, aggressive, and unmanageable. They would be injected with insulin until they went into an induced coma for a few days, they were monitored closely and their melancholia, as they called it would pass. Iced baths were used too, which seemed really inhumane, but the shock seemed to have a similar effect.

Years before these treatments patients were whipped until they were exhausted and could fight no more, all of these treatments were used in the last century before they had developed drugs to sedate people. Convulsive therapy was first started in St Brendan's in 1938. This was quite crude, at that time as there was an anesthetic but no muscle relaxant used, and when a patient was having a fit they often had fractures bones, it was known as a straight or unmodified form of ECT.

The modern form of Elective Convulsive Therapy, ECT, is much safer and more refined, for patients and sometimes is used when all drug therapies fail. I have seen it work for many patients in my career. In 1938, neuroleptics formerly known as major tranquilizers were first introduced into psychiatry, so the need for physical restraint was not used often. Thank god I said to myself that treatments were much better in my time, as I could not see myself partaking in the older treatments.

I suppose at the time they had no other way of treating the mentally ill. There was not enough research or studies on the human mind, it's the hardest, most baffling thing to understand, the human mind. We often see it with people who take their own lives, we expect to see some signs, but often there are none. And to this day we see people who seem perfectly fine getting on with life, suddenly deciding to end it. The mind is so fascinating and the most concealed part of the body, often people tell us what they want us to hear, not what they are really thinking or feeling. Suicide leaves relatives and friends bewildered, devastated, they rack their brains, thinking they should have noticed changes in mood, habits, behaviour, but sometimes there are no answers. It is so important to talk to people and support them if you ever have the slightest inkling something might be troubling someone, but as I said sometimes we just don't know and can't prevent it, and if we are lucky, sometimes we can.

I have had the experience of many people taking their own lives: doctors, nurses, sons, daughters, and relatives, loved ones in families we knew. All we could do was support them in their grief, and in St Brendan's when something happened to staff or staff's relatives we always rallied around as we were a family and still are. Mental health awareness is so important, it affects everyone, young and old, rich or poor. And it is great to see actors, singers, film stars, sports people, and people from every walk of life raising awareness about mental health issues.

It is only in the last decade that people feel brave enough to publicly speak about mental health, and all other health conditions that were taboo in the past. Mental health issues affect everyone, from older people with dementia, depression, and Alzheimer's, to younger people with anorexia, poor self-image, self-harming, inability to cope, addiction to alcohol or drugs or gambling, mothers with postpartum depression, gender identification, to people of any age who can't face life, and decide to end it. So we all must promote mental health issues and lobby our ministers and all government officials to tackle these issues with staff, resources, and funding.

The older nurses had some very serious but funny stories too, if nurses misbehaved they would be sent on the blue bus to Portrane. One nurse I worked with told me that as a student she was accompanying a patient who was to be transferred there. As St Brendan's was getting overcrowded, and Portrane had vacancies. In those days poor patients with no one to vouch for them had no say in the matter.

So off she went with the patient in the blue bus and delivered the patient to the assigned ward, however the driver was instructed by the matron to return without the nurse, and she was assigned to do duty there for a month. When she inquired about her transport back to St Brendan's, she was told she was to be given a room in the nurses' home, and her uniforms and belongings would be delivered the next day, apparently this happened to quite a few nurses, male and female. We laugh now about the punishments that were dished out, but the power the Matron and the Chief Male nurse had at the time, was not questioned.

I was very surprised when reading Dr Ivor Browne's book "Music and Madness" to learn that Dr Dunne had sent him to St Ita's for a month, to get more experience of what life was like in St Ita's. He was not impressed, but probably learned a lot, as St Ita's was quite isolated at that time if you had no transport, but it also had the luxury of being by the sea, you could walk around the cliffs by the sea. He might have spent many evenings there contemplating and playing his tin whistle and seeing what life was like there as opposed to city living in St Brendan's. He said he was glad to get back to St Brendan's, bad and all as he thought it was.

In a lot of hospitals around the country the patients who were well enough were brought out to farms to work. It was deemed therapy for them, and indeed it was good to be out in the fresh air all day rather than being in a stuffy ward with nothing to do. Some people might say this practice was abused in some places, but from my childhood experience, I can remember my father, who was a psychiatric nurse, bringing one patient who he trusted to work on our farm at home on some of his days off. His name was Tony, a gentle person, and he had his lunch and tea with us as part of the family. He loved working on the farm and looked forward to my father's days off when he would bring him to work with him on the farm. One day Tony was very anxious, he was having a panic attack, my dad was worried as I was walking towards him. I was four at that time, before my dad could reach me I had taken Tony's hand and he completely calmed down, my dad couldn't believe it. He scooped me into his arms and told me years later what I just said to him, "Tony was afraid," I just held his hand to make him better.

St Ita's Hospital was established in Portrane in 1901, it stood on seventy acres of land, out on the peninsula of North County Dublin beside the sea and supplied St Brendan's with all its fruit and vegetables as it was prime land for crop development.

It's amazing that in later years when all the farming activities were closed, the authorities had to employ occupational therapists to occupy patients in useful and enjoyable activities which had been previously done by nurses as well as their nursing duties. The scope for activities and space was very limited, therapies were set up in hospitals all over the country to occupy patients during the day, and it seemed hard for the occupational therapists to take over roles that nurses, despite all their other duties had done for decades.

In St Brendan's there was an OT department specifically set up so that patients could leave their units and spend the day in activities. This therapy was run by nurses with staff with specific skills. The printing department was excellent and the carpentry department. I got an easel made for my own artwork which I still use. I bought stools to sit on, that the patients made and a beautiful embroidery picture, that one particular lady was excellent at doing. I treasure these items and will pass them on to my children as they are all handmade and one-off pieces.

They had a sale every year and the money generated went back into the therapy unit to purchase new materials. They also took on contracts packing boxes, envelopes etc., and the patients were paid accordingly for their day's work. It was in this occupational therapy that all the Gateway and St Brendan's magazines were printed from 1968 to 1974. These magazines included any developments in the hospital, news of nurses going to do their general nursing in England, new babies being born, and letters and poems from patients, news of anyone getting engaged or married, a history of ST Brendan's, and a sports section on St Brendan's and St Ita's every month.

We worked while we studied and as exams approached, we would study in small groups. We formed deeper friendships. I remember one night the lads, our pals, stood outside the nurses' home with chips. We obviously couldn't come out, so we sent down a rope and they attached the bags of chips for us to help with the studies. We enjoyed our social outlets, when we got out and life was hectic. Our training was incorporated into our working schedule with two weeks four times a year set aside, where we were in the school of nursing, away from working on the wards. Our curriculum was designed to incorporate both theory and nursing practise, theory in the school of nursing, and nursing practise, which was graded on the wards by the nurse in charge, who hopefully you got on with. We had a booklet with all the skills we had to pass at each term of our practise.

The picture made by one of the patients.

Some charge nurses were very good and encouraging, while others were indifferent and found students more of a nuisance than a help. Some charge nurses felt it just added more work and responsibility to their roles, and they often delegated these duties to staff nurses. I found most nurses helpful in explaining symptoms, behaviours and mannerisms of patients relating to their different diagnosis, physical diseases, and many different disorders. I remember arriving in a geriatric unit, Unit G with forty patients, and the staff nurse said to me, listen, "these patients all have dementia, or pre-senile dementia", very broad diagnosis, but she felt she covered everything with that statement. She said, "Its busy enough here without you asking all these questions," so that's it; they all have dementia end of.

The charge nurse, who was in her late forties or early fifties, had got engaged. She was flashing her ring at the tea break, and she said, "Girls, what do you think?"

"Congratulations," I said, and my co-worker said, "better late than never." I kicked her under the table, she copped on and congratulated her. The work was hard enough we didn't want her breathing down our necks all day, so congratulations on her engagement was essential just to keep her happy. I was genuinely delighted for her, to have a partner and not to live her life alone. She was so happy, she was like a teenager again.

I suppose the diagnosis the staff nurse gave us was correct, and it was more advanced than the diagnosis of lunatic, which we found in a lot of the charts, we stumbled on this one day in the top of the building called the Annexe, the back of the building, which obviously we were not to have any access, but we bided our time, and when it was quiet, we actually found our pass key unlocked the door, and we searched through the old charts. I was fascinated by the physical details in the charts, a photograph of the person, their height, weight, eye colour, a map of any injuries, mental state, e.g., manic, confused, disorientated, withdrawn etc.

We spent hours in the top of the annexe looking through the charts which were not very well kept and pigeons flying in and out. After all that, the majority if not all the diagnoses were lunatic. Most of the entries by the psychiatrist were only every six months after the initial assessment. I thought this was very laxed, you could be on the same cocktail of medicine for six months, and if there was no outbursts or difficult behaviour, you were not seen again until your six monthly review. These reviews according to the notes were very short as in, "doing fine" and, continuing current regime. It would have been great at the time to have a mobile phone just to get one picture of one chart.

As a student nurse, you never got to look at the charts except on night duty as you were in charge, imagine student nurses in charge of a unit at night time on your own, mostly geriatric units. A nurse from an adjoining unit would come at night and in the early morning to assist you in changing the patients, who were bedridden and needed changing and turning their position to prevent bedsores. Patients were checked and changed three times during the night. We had some rotary beds, which constantly rolled the patient gently like rocking them from one side to the other. There was a great record in St Brendan's of the absence of bedsores. If someone was admitted with one, it was quickly treated. Our worst nightmare would be some patient having to go to general hospital, when they would arrive back with bedsores and we would have to start the healing process again.

We were very good at healing bed sores, constant changing of dressings, and above all moving the patient every hour if severe or two hours if not so severe, no pressure was to be allowed on the pressure sore area. One morning when the charge nurse had gone to her breakfast at 8 a.m. when the rest of the staff came on duty, my friend said to me, "I wonder what it's like to lie in that rotary bed all day," I said, "Try it." We had to take the lady in it for a bath, so the nurse got in. I put the sides up and turned it on, just then we heard a key in the door, it was the deputy matron on her rounds. She said, "Get me out," I said we don't have time just stay there, if she is looking for you, I'll tell her you are gone next door to borrow sheets.

So I covered her up when the deputy matron asked me where is your second nurse? I explained she had to borrow some sheets, she passed through the ward, and I let the nurse out. She said, "Oh my god that was close."

I said, "What was it like anyway?"

She said, "It was cosy and snug, but so boring just looking at the ceiling all day and night."

So we decided to put a radio near her bed so at least she could listen to music. Another nurse on this unit was asked by the charge nurse to clean all the patient's dentures, so she collected the dentures, put them all in a big bowl of sterilizing fluid, and cleaned them. She forgot to put them in individual containers, so she spent the rest of the day finding out which dentures belonged to which patient. We never told the charge nurse of course.

We did our preliminary exams in our first year of training. I passed. Some people who did not pass could repeat three times, then we did our final exams in our third year. It was a good system of training as we were working on the wards, day duty, and night duty which gave us great opportunities to link the patients' symptoms to the various diseases physical, psychological, and mental illnesses. We would study at night time when the patients were attended to, as well as our designated weeks in the school away from the wards.

I remember one-night duty in particular when I was assigned to Unit 7, the secure unit a staff nurse and I were assigned to "special" a particular patient (that meant the person had to be closely observed), there were no rooms with cameras fitted at that time, this would come several years later, where you could observe the patient from another room or office. This patient who was very psychotic, in fact I don't think I have ever seen anyone so psychotic. We had to sit outside her single room in a cold corridor, with no heating on, so we had to keep warm with a blanket wrapped over our soldiers and around our knees. The ledges on the window in her room were very deep like a window seat, she would not get into her bed, and spent the night on the ledge, with her hair standing straight up from her head, her eyes rolling back into her head then glaring at us again. She only spoke to scream at us, we had a job to pacify her, she was so troubled, we tried to calm her but if you went near her it was quite dangerous. When I think about it now, when she would stand up on the ledge, we backed away as we knew the next thing that would happen is that she would jump on one of us and you would not get her off you, so we let her be.

We would be called up to the office for our midnight tea break, which we really looked forward to, as there was only one TV in the sitting room, which was off at night. We could not sit there either as we had to be near the patients, we might just get to read a book if the patient was asleep. Two other nurses would take over the watch until we got back. The office was cosy and warm, one night we went in and the nurse in charge had a camogie stick. She was standing at the fireplace waiting for something, we sat down at the table to have our supper, the next thing this half drunken rat appeared from a hole at the side of the fireplace. She swung the camogie stick and said, "That's No. 3 tonight," and put the rat in a sack. I was dumbfounded, I wouldn't have believed it only I witnessed it myself. She said she would have a few more by morning.

There was rat poison put down discreetly in various areas around the unit, and on another night duty in that unit, I was sent to Jervis St Hospital in town with a patient who deliberately, regularly swallowed the rat poison. Jervis street was a busy general hospital with all the facilities, just off O'Connell Street, Jervis street hospital later amalgamated with the Richmond General Hospital, which is now Beaumont Hospital. This lady had a habit of doing this and every time she went to Jervis St Hospital, the doctor would give her something to make her sick and vomit, so every other night when I arrived on night duty, I would ask her before I had my break, did you swallow any rat poison tonight or anything else.

I was sick of watching her retching and getting sick, she was so used to getting attention with this behaviour, and the doctors in Jervis Street were so sick of attending to her every night. My last trip out with her, the fourth night that week, we met the same doctor, she was on the couch screaming her head off and would not take the medicine. I tried to calm her with no luck, so the doctor looked at me and said, "She's hysterical."

I said, "I couldn't agree more," so he gave her a hard slap

across the face. She was so shocked she stayed still and immediately took the medicine.

The doctor said, "Well done, and I do not want to see you here tomorrow night. I actually need to attend to people who are actually sick." When I thought of it later that night, I laughed that was one way of curing this behaviour. I never had to go out with her again for the rest of the night duty, but she resumed these behaviours over time.

I got home from time to time on night duty leave or holidays. Life was still pretty busy for my family at home, my father worked in the local psychiatric hospital and had a fruit farm and animals to care for on his days off to make ends meet. There were twelve of us, six boys and six girls. My mother and all of us played a large part in the running of the farm, especially during picking season, with daily runs with fruit to the co-op twelve miles away in Carrickmacross after leaving the pickers' home. I helped out as much as possible when I went home. I bought clothes for my younger brothers out of my small wages.

When I got home I used to scrub the house from top to bottom, I knew my mother had little time for housekeeping with all the work she had to do on the farm, and she did do the important things. I remember her baking every day, we always had fresh brown bread, scones, fruit and ginger cakes and homemade jam. My mother was great at making ends meet. She made clothes, had a sewing and knitting machine, we all received new knitted jumpers every year, two or three each, especially before Christmas. My mother had little help except from us, and believe me, we learned to look after our younger brothers and sisters.

When I lived at home, one of my sisters and I were told to take the youngest babies for walks down the bog for hours to give my mother a break. The kids loved it of course and slept soundly from all the fresh air and exercise. I remember we had the two youngest strapped into a deep pram and we would go up the bog road, one of us at the top and the other at the bottom. Then we would let the pram off down the hill, the babies thought this was great and kept asking, "Again, again," we could spend a few hours doing this game. God knows what health and safety would say now, but they were secure and no harm ever came to them.

Mother always made every birthday special. We always had our chocolate cake, little fairy cakes and could invite our special friends. As we got older and wanted some music, the radio was all that was available. We could use the hay shed for a bit of crack. My mother used to enter the Gael Linn Pools. One year when we were young she won, we begged her to buy a television. They were very expensive at the time, with three stations RTE, UTV and BBC. She relented and spent the money on the TV, our house became very popular with neighbours, and children sneaking in to have a peek and watch a film.

We had a long sofa at the end of the sitting room, and when my mother was cooking of course we had to mind the baby in the pram, we used to tie a rope onto the pram, give it a kick with our foot and shove it up and down the sitting room while watching the TV, the baby always slept then. We grew up all minding each other, we had plenty of experience minding babies with all our younger brothers and sisters. Time passed and we were soon teenagers doing as teenagers do, going to the pictures, roller skating in the church hall and going to dances in the Adelphi Ballroom in Dundalk, the Nuremore Hotel in Carrickmacross. I remember one night as we were ready to go, we had our miniskirts and white leather boots on, just as we were going out the door, my dad said, "My god those skirts are very short, they look like a belt."

I said, "Sure they are all the rage now."

He said, "Go on you'll do what you want to do anyway".

My father loved my mother very much, he used to write her little letters as phones were few and far between. We probably got our house phone because of my father's union work as he had to be contactable. Believe me, he certainly spent hours on the phone at night after a long shift, trying to solve people's problems and dilemmas. He was always so busy with his nurses' work, being a union official, and he was also involved in setting up a co-op, Fane Valley co-op, for farmers in the area to sell their produce in a factory in Carrickmacross. He was very interested in this, as we had a fruit and vegetable farm.

Sometimes when he would come home from work on bright evenings, he would go out on the tractor and plough the fields, he said it was relaxing after a day in a psychiatric ward. Whenever I did visit home my mother always had a goody bag for me to take back to the hospital, which we enjoyed for a week or so: cake, scones, homemade brown bread, and jams of all sorts for our night-time treats. We did have a kettle in our rooms, which we had to buy ourselves of course, but it was a wise investment and well used. My friends would call to my room at night for tea and a chat, I was reported to the home sister once or twice for noise with the girls chatting and laughing it was harmless, the deputy matron who lived opposite me complained, so I ended up having to apologize to her to keep the peace.

We did our preliminary exams in our first year of training, I passed. Some people who did not pass could repeat three times over the next two years. We gained a lot of experience in our own hospital in the upper house and the lower house. In second year, we were seconded to a general hospital for three months as part of our training. There were three hospitals we could be sent to: The Richmond Hospital, The Meath Hospital, and The Adelaide Hospital. I was so lucky to be sent to The Richmond Hospital as I could literally go through the grounds of the lower house, and there was a gate on a pass key and a road to The Richmond Hospital. The other two hospitals were on the south side of the city and involved getting busses etc.

Richmond Hospital

The general hospitals were a really different kind of nursing than we were used to. Patients were going for operations, or recovering from them, or waiting on tests or results. It was very task orientated, students spent lots of time in the sluice rooms emptying and cleaning bedpans. We might get to listen in on a ward round when consultants visited with their entourage of medical students. We were given a lot of responsibility too.

In the evening you were to take charge of wards with a staff nurse or sister calling in from time to time. While on placement in Richmond, I remember being asked by the charge nurse to help this gentleman to have a bath, he just had an operation for piles and had to soak in a salt bath for fifteen minutes for a few days after the operation. I said ok. We would not have had to bathe male patients in our hospital as the wards or staff were not mixed. We would go into the bathroom, he stripped off, and I would have to help him into the bath. He was embarrassed, I certainly was, but I said to myself you're a professional so act like it.

He said to me, "You must see this every day."

I said, "Of course." Little did he know we had not worked on male wards, so I had to just get on with the job. He thanked me, and I said no problem all part of a day's work. We had to spend a morning in the mortuary as part of our placement. I didn't know what to expect, a little baby girl was in the morgue, her milk bottle still in her hand. I presumed she choked but I will never know they never told you, but that picture was etched in my mind. Another corpse was of a young man lying on the next slab, just the same age as my boyfriend, I thought, *what a waste dying so young.* You never heard how they died as coroners' reports would take months at that time to process, it's not much different now.

There was another lady in a ward long term, as there had been a mistake with her surgery. She had one leg that was gangerous and had to be removed, but in surgery they removed the wrong leg, the hospital took responsibility for her and gave her space in a ward. She was bed bound, and very grumpy with the result that no one wanted to attend to her. I used to talk to her in the evenings and she always requested I give her, her injection for pain, I was very direct with her not giving in to her complaints which I think she appreciated, everyone else was tiptoeing around her. My last evening there she asked for me as usual, I gave her the injection and she said she had a present for me. I told her we couldn't accept presents but she insisted, I said goodbye, gave her a hug, I felt so sorry for her. There was no plan for her only to be nursed in that ward, her only outlet was reading books and for the six weeks I was there I never saw anyone visiting her. I brought her books from the library ones she had not read, she was so grateful for the books, she was let down very badly by the service. I wished I could do more for her but I was going back to St Brendan's and would not hear from her again. When I got back to the nurses home, I opened the present, it was an expensive bottle of perfume. Our last week in the general hospital was to observe some operations in theater, I just wanted to see a few operations first hand unfortunately due to staff shortages I was called back to St Brendan's. I was actually glad to get back, there was such a hierarchical system in general nursing. A second year student could tell a first year what to do, a third year telling the second years what to do and so on, you could just leave your brain at the door, and what I really didn't miss was the uniform inspection every morning fifteen minutes before your shift, if you had a hair out of place you had to pin it up. So we all carried clips and pins in our pockets.

I decided there and then after my time in a general hospital that psychiatry was for me, while it was a more dangerous working environment. It was more exciting and interesting, and often physical symptoms present as a result of mental trauma. I was then sent to Cherry Orchard Hospital to special a young adult female who was transferred there for physical reasons. I had never been to Cherry Orchard Hospital before, eventually I found the patient. I was a bit dumbfounded at the state she was in, there was a handcuff on her wrist and ankle attached to the bed to keep her in it. I was given no history or handover about her condition. The charge nurse came in after thirty minutes. I tried to calm her, stroking her head, asked her if she was in pain, she nodded that she was. I said to the charge nurse she needs a doctor immediately, she is so agitated because she is in pain. She looked at me as if to say what do you know, but she got the doctor who agreed with me and gave her an injection for pain, she settled. I found out she was there because she had an infection and was in isolation she was delirious, which was mistaken for psychiatric symptoms. I was not informed of her condition, she was asleep so I went to find the sister to ask if she was been barrier nursed, and could I have a mask, apron, and gloves. She got me the equipment and got the patient charted for regular pain relief with her IV antibiotics. I spent six nights there, and she improved. During the weekend she was pleasant and chatting. I asked them to take the handcuffs off while I was there and to be fair to her, she didn't try to escape. I brought her magazines and books to keep her busy until she was well.

After three years of working and studying, in 1975 we sat our written exams, did our oral exams and thankfully passed and joined the ranks of staff nurses. Our fee at that time was £4. 25 which we had to pay to sit our exams. Then you were called a medal nurse as you got your medal on qualification.

St Brendan and Bord Altranais medals

My graduation and some of my classmates who graduated too.

We had to go to Arnott's in Henry Street to get our new white uniforms. It was great although they were very expensive as were the nurses' shoes. I was very proud to wear my hospital badge, it was a symbol of achievement, and we worked very hard to get it. I was asked by the Director of nursing one morning if I would go to the Irish hospitals' sweepstakes the next day with a group of other nurses throughout the country it was held in Ballsbridge. I said yes but I would have to get my hair done. He said, "Ask the ward sister for an extended lunch break," so I did. I just went to Manor Street which was local, I was waiting in the salon when a patient in the ward who had her liberty spotted me, she was next in line but she said to the stylist, "Let my nurse go first, she's on her break, I'm in no rush," fair play to her. I was embarrassed as everyone looked around. I got the hair done, all set for the sweepstake. The Irish sweepstake was a lottery to fund hospitals at that time, it was a privilege to be asked, but a very tiring day as we had to rehearse several times, and hopefully I brought someone some luck.

As soon as we qualified we were asked to take charge in the units, if charge nurses were on holidays and there was no relief nurse to take over for the week or two weeks, as the marriage bar was still in situ and senior married nurses had to forgo promotion, and younger and sometimes newly qualified nurses like us were given this task. This was pretty terrifying for us as we had no experience of being in charge of units except on night duty, day duty was a completely different kettle of fish.

My first assignment as acting charge was to unit number 7, a three-storey block built with pure granite consisting of units 2, 4, 6, 8, and 7, the dreaded high secure unit in the upper house which consisted of single rooms at each end of the unit, and a large dormitory in the middle and a sitting room at each end.

Unfortunately this building was demolished in later years as part of the closure of the hospital, we were all devastated as it again was a beautiful aesthetic looking building on the outside. The decor and the condition of the building on the inside was rarely upgraded to the necessary standard for patients to live and nurses to work in, it was always the same story "the Health Board had no money." The granite blocks were so difficult to demolish, special equipment had to be sourced by the Health Board to do this, and then the granite blocks were transported abroad to Sweden for sale. It was such a pity to lose that building, the health board must have got a lot of money for the granite but of course this information was never made public.

I had only been on night duty Unit 7 as a student, and now I was been assigned to take charge of it. This unit was so large it was very difficult to keep things running smoothly. We were warned by the senior nurses, especially the girls I lived with, never to go anywhere in this unit on your own, to go in twos as you were likely to be attacked by some well-known characters who seemed resistant to medication for their particular illness. I remember one lady in particular who would jump on any nurse who was on their own, so we all quickly got to know the ropes to keep as safe as we could. We set about our daily tasks of feeding, washing and medicating patients, all of these tasks were very difficult with this group of people. As the unit was mixed with all age groups, young and some older women, women who were pregnant, intellectual disability with behavioural problems, women with schizophrenia, manic depression or bipolar as it is now described.

Some of these women needed to be secluded in their rooms for their safety, or the safety of the other patients and staff. They would be prescribed sedation by their consultant or registrar which was administered by the nursing staff, on these occasions the patient would be offered oral medication but if they refused, which they usually did in these extremely agitated or psychotic states, or if the person was very manic, and threatening, or high as we used to call it. So this took the form of gentle persuasion which sometimes worked if you had a good repour with the patient, but sometimes they were too disturbed to listen to anybody, they would run frantically around the ward often hitting other vulnerable patients and staff too, so then we just had to safely hold the patient down on their bed to administer the medication safely by intramuscular injections.

When patients were in seclusion in single rooms we had to keep hourly checks to ensure their safety, and again two or three of us would go into the room to check, we did not have the luxury of cameras for years later so everything had to be done manually. In some single rooms it was too dangerous for the patient to have a bed there was always the possibility of choking themselves between the bars, or strangling themselves with a garment, so in these cases they slept on a mat on the floor, other patients who were extremely disturbed would be in a strait jacket for a while to prevent injury to themselves until the medication began to take effect and they would calm down. Bathing was again difficult, no patient was allowed have a bath on their own. It was a suicide risk, drown in a bath, we did not have showers then until a later date.

When I was assigned to this high secure unit, the dreaded Unit 7, I certainly relied on my senior colleagues for advice and direction, and made our working day as pleasant as possible for staff and patients. Some nurses when given charge of a unit, acted in an authoritarian manner, caused grave resentment from senior staff who were much more qualified in nursing, and had years of experience behind them. I had the wisdom not to fall into that trap and constantly valued their direction and experience. Nursing was much harder for senior staff having to endure junior nurses, just qualified being in charge, they were overlooked for promotion just because they got married, the marriage bar was not lifted for years later, I often felt they would be really frustrated and annoyed with this situation of some young whippersnapper just qualified being in charge, they managed to keep cool in very difficult times, and I really admired them.

Our new responsibilities as acting charge nurses was very daunting. We were thrown into management without any training, and even though we had the support of the senior nurses, that is, if they liked us, and had a good working relationship with them, I had to make the final decision on many matters. Most of the wards had routines, some were necessary but some were very strict in relation to patients in the secure units "the block" as we called it, the mix of patients meant some were psychopathic, sociopathic, schizophrenic, patients who suffered from depression, acute and endogenous, or bi-polar in today's terminology, and some patients with intellectual disability. This mixture was disastrous as their needs were so different, and nurses had very few resources to keep these patients safe and find time to occupy them. Nurses were very resourceful people, they formed small groups, with games, knitting, painting, games even playing toys for those with intellectual disability.

All nursing duties were ongoing and outpatient appointments in general hospitals with constant visits, were a constant drain on the nursing staff, appointments in general hospitals could take hours, with patients who had cut themselves badly, or managed to take overdoses, or many patients had a habit of swallowing glass, batteries, spoons, knives, rat poison to name but a few. Nurses were on constant vigils, often relatives or acquaintances managed to get drugs to patients through small windows, or visitors, visiting patients were clever at hiding medication in their clothing giving it to patients. You could not search relatives at the door, it was a hospital after all and not a prison. These attempts to smuggle in medication to patients were seldom, but they did happen. Nurses could not just hand a patient medication and expect them to take it, you had to stay with them and make sure they swallowed the tablets, and not hide them under their tongues as many would try to do. Bathing was a chore. Our supplies came in five litre containers of bath gels and shampoo. We did however always have plenty of creams and powders for cuts or sores or wounds. I survived my few weeks as an acting charge in Unit 7 thanks to the senior nurses.

Nurses were very consistent in their efforts to ensure that no patient got bed sores. In my time in the geriatric units patients were turned from one position to another, washed and creamed seven times a day and three times at night, so in psychiatric hospitals bed sores were very rare, and if any did occur on a newly admitted patient they were rapidly treated. Meals and nutrition was a must if someone could not eat on their own, like the older men and women in the geriatric units, they were spoon fed all of their meals and supplemented with nutrients such as complan, and other nutritional drinks and formulas, the nursing care in the geriatric units was second to none.

It was more difficult to maintain nutrition in other units such as the admission units, and the secure units, because of the mixture of patients some of whom also had anorexia, or had been physically or sexually abused, so eating was not high on their agenda. Nurses had to observe closely at patient meals and if someone with anorexia left the dining room a nurse had to follow them to see if they were vomiting up their meal as they often did. Patients with anorexia were very hard to treat. We would make every effort to get them what they might eat, leave little treats for them in the hope they might eat something, but some of them had such a distorted view of their body image it took a long time in recovery. Not all of them recovered enough to lead a normal life and were often admitted again.

Some of the ladies who were pregnant had no properly fitting clothes, so my friends and I used to bring in all our maternity wear that we had, to keep them comfortable. Most of these ladies had no relatives or they did not visit. Some babies were born in the hospital due to the unknown date of expectancy, and were transferred to the rotunda or St James Hospital. Another night on night duty, I was in an admission unit where a lady who was not suspected of being pregnant went into labour, I was on my round of the ward with my torch, and I could hear all this groaning. It was Susie who had intellectual disability and was not very good at communicating. I asked her what was wrong she pointed to her stomach, and boy was I shocked we did not even know she was pregnant, she was very slim. I pulled back the covers and it was obvious to me she was in labour her waters had broken, she was terrified, she didn't know what was happening. I reassured her and said I was going to get the other nurse and call the duty doctor.

We called an ambulance and another nurse from the assessment unit to help, she came running in she wanted to be there for the delivery, but the little baby girl was born and gone in the ambulance, She was livid she missed the excitement, but this baby was not waiting for anyone, she just slipped out. She was tiny but perfectly formed, I wrapped her in a soft blanket, and it was so quick even the duty doctor missed it. We had a brilliant consultant gynaecologist Dr Hanratty who had a baby clinic once a month for any of our patients who were pregnant. He also gave us pregnant nurses a consultation to save us the journey of going to St James. My friend Teresa used to operate these clinics with Dr Hanratty, I had all my babies in St James's, in hospital five under his care, that unit was closed after I had my last son in 1986.

A few years prior to that I was calling for my friend Teresa, she was working in Unit O at the time. She was due to go on maternity leave and invited me down to her house as usual. I was just outside the unit when she came out, just as we were going out the front gate her waters broke. I panicked and said, "Will I go back in to the unit and phone your husband?"

"No," she said. "It's only five minutes down the road, keep going."

We got to the house, I ran in to get him, he said, "Stay with the kids, we need to go to hospital." So I did. I got them all to bed, went to bed myself, and the next morning he arrived back at 6.30 announcing they had a baby boy, all was well.

Psychiatric hospitals and mental health services were never high on the agenda for the government or ministers for health as we had learned from the past. We strove constantly through our unions. The Irish Transport and General Workers Union, now known as SIPTU, and The Psychiatric Nurses Union, and the Workers Union of Ireland, to improve conditions for patients and their treatments, and also to improve working conditions and health and safety conditions for nurses. From the 1980s onwards there was always a shortage of staff, with nurses being sent from one ward to another on several occasions. Management's solution was to allow nurses and auxiliary staff to do overtime to fill the vacancies, but this too ceased in 1982 with a directive from the minister for health and the government.

Consultants had their own regime of treatments depending on which consultant the patient's care was provided, nurses would know what each particular consultant would usually prescribe. The consultants had their own areas of responsibility, this was decided by catchment areas. St Brendan's covered all areas of the city, north side, south side, and inner city, plus anyone arriving from the airport who arrived into Ireland mentally unwell, would automatically go to St Brendan's. Anyone arriving into Ireland by boat was the responsibility of St Ita's hospital when it opened. We had several au pairs arriving in Ireland, and others who genuinely needed treatment, the services were very mixed, there were no specialized units for psychiatric, mentally handicapped, or as we now refer to these people as intellectual disability. Ladies with anorexia and postpartum depression, my heart went out to all these different people as they were all together in units with very psychotic patients, patients with schizophrenia and depression and other mixed diagnosis.

I remember one night on night duty in a long stay ward, during the night we got a call to take an admission. We were expecting an older lady but this beautiful young woman arrived, distressed and tearful, she had postpartum depression, her baby was only a few days old. My heart went out to her but we had to keep her safe. She had tried to harm herself and her baby, she thought she had killed her baby. It's hard to imagine at that time that you would end up in a psychiatric unit among long stay patients after having a baby. There were no services for her only this. She had been given some sedation thank god to calm her down. I got her into bed, I explained it was only for the night.

They had no beds in the admission unit, we kept a very close eye on her all night, as she was suicidal, as well as minding all the other patients. I said goodbye to her in the morning gave her a cup of tea and asked her to try and rest, she would be transferred to the admission unit, and she was. It was so difficult for her to see where she was that night, she was terrified, and I reassured her that we would look after her, that she would see her baby that her baby was alive. I explained to her that this sometimes happens after having a baby, but we had to keep her and her baby safe for now, she was safe. My sister who worked in St Davnet's in Monaghan told me that when mothers were admitted there with postpartum depression that mothers were allowed to bring their babies into hospital with them, so the nurses had to mind the mothers and babies. Thank god those services have come a long way and nowadays, this would not happen to any unfortunate mother with postpartum depression.

Psychiatric nurses got the opportunity to see and nurse people with medical conditions as well as psychiatric conditions, so we were researching all these different conditions. Our knowledge base broadened and I can honestly say that there were very few illnesses unknown to us, the expertise of nurses was undervalued and we had to nurse these people, some with multiple sclerosis, Huntington's chorea, brain injuries from accidents, Prader Willie syndrome, this is a rare genetic disorder that results in a number of physical, mental and behavioural problems. A key feature is a constant sense of hunger that starts at approximately two years of age.

We had one such lady admitted as she had been in a home

until she was eighteen. Then she was admitted to St Brendan's because there was nowhere else where she could be treated, she was with us for three years before she died on a trip to Lourdes. She was quite hard to observe she would hide food in her pockets in the dining room, so she had to be observed at all times. She was moody and nurses had to coax her to attend to personal hygiene, etc. She was a very obese lady and had very little clothes to fit her for her trip to Lourdes. The charge nurse knew I was handy with the sewing machine and asked me to make her some clothes for the trip. I went into Hickeys in town at my lunch break and got material. I made her some dresses and nightgowns for the holiday to Lourdes. She was delighted, we sent her off, she was happy, but unfortunately she passed away in Rome, I was glad I was able to help her.

There were patients with all the different forms of dementia, in the most difficult of units which were not designed appropriately. It was not until the mid-eighties that attempts were made, to place people with intellectual disability in St Ita's Hospital in Portrane Co Dublin, where specialist nurses were trained in the management of patients with intellectual disability, the services in St Ita's were divided to the Psychiatric side, and the Intellectual disability side. I later learned when I was accepted promotion as Assistant Director of Nursing in St Ita's, the nurses referred to the intellectual disability side as the far side. I actually thought at first that they meant people had passed on to the other side, heaven.

On the social side, many couples met and married from relationships formed in St Brendan's, and many relationships broke up and people separated too, like in every walk of life. We were near Dublin city centre. Our lives were here now, where we worked and lived, a few nurses got transfers back to their home towns where there were psychiatric hospitals. A few nurses in my group soon learned they were not cut out for psychiatry, as they found it too challenging and applied for general nursing. There were rules and regulations of course, at that time, you could only get a transfer if you were still a student nurse, I did not want a transfer home because my dad was working in the local hospital which was very strict at that time.

I also felt I would be working in his shadow and not allowed to develop my own lifestyle. He was a union official at the time (SIPTU) and made great changes for nurses' and patients' rights. He was a charge nurse in a challenging unit where he made changes for the patients, he got some homely items, pictures on the walls, a newspaper daily, better seating, and arts and crafts for those patients who had to stay in the ward, who were not allowed to go out. He continued to do this all of his life often having less time to spend with his family, but the union was his passion and all it stood for, my mother was happy he had this outlet. He was a teetotaller, so his nights were often spent at union meetings in the local catchment areas, and meetings in liberty hall in Dublin, or many hours on the phone sorting out members' problems and dilemmas. My father and his union colleagues fought for nurses' rights, increased annual leave, pay increases, representing nurses and auxiliary staff in the labour relations commission, and representing staff at a local level to try and resolve individual issues that needed attention.

The staff canteen was a revelation for some staff, most of the younger nurses would be sent to the first dinner so new staff and qualified staff could suss out new recruits, like us. The charge nurses used to go to second dinner so one could imagine the assumptions and chatter about us, so there was always a buzz and an air of curiosity at meal times, the canteen staff were very thoughtful and courteous, back then our dinner was served to us, and they always gave extra portions to growing lads. The speculation of pregnancies among young new staff was high on the agenda as there was not much in the line of contraception, in fact, if you even wanted condoms you had to get them in the north of Ireland, or from England.

One senior married nurse told me if she felt like sex, she and her husband would say the rosary. I told her that we said the rosary at home for years as was the custom, in many homes, but it never worked for my mother and father, after all I was one of twelve children. Another senior nurse said to me after she had two children, she said to her husband, "Do you see that tree in the garden? Drill a big hole in it and help yourself, I'm off limits." I thought that was a bit crude, I could never imagine me saying that to my husband, he was never very handy at DIY and we didn't have a tree. So we had to find ways around this issue too, as hormones were flying, we were young and active people, and naturally things were going to happen.

Some nurses would get pregnant, have babies and have them adopted, these happenings were all kept under wraps in the past. We heard stories of nurses having babies in secret in the nurses' home, the older nurses never elaborated on what arrangements were made for these babies, but in my time some nurses kept their babies, some had them adopted, and some had them fostered until they were in a position to care for them, and work in the meantime, and some people got married. These times were so hard and sad for those nurses and they often had no choice, but to give up their babies, especially living in Dublin, or major cities, as rents were so high, and the standard of accommodation was not vetted and often appalling.

For those who managed to keep their babies, it was a great triumph, there was not very much support for single mothers, to keep your baby and continue your education, but for those who gave up their babies for adoption, making the ultimate sacrifice for their babies future, it made many families so happy, to have a beautiful child to love and cherish as they could not have their own. Those mothers were doing the best for their child, and made very brave decisions, and the hardest decisions they would ever have to make, to give their baby to a home and two loving parents who really wanted them.

I managed to survive until I got married, that was the plan. We dated for four years before we married. My boyfriend was very passionate and loving and always had my best interest at heart, we used to meet every night, except for one night a week where he insisted I should have a girl's night to keep up with my friends. When I first moved to flatland with my friend who didn't want to stay in the nurses' home for personal reasons, it was tough, that one bedroom double bedsit, with a corned-off kitchen, and a shared toilet and shower on the landing outside, there was a list at the bathroom door that you had to sign if you wanted to book a shower, it was very cramped and not at all what I would have been used to growing up on a farm, with a few acres of land.

We stayed there for a few months and then she decided to move out to another flat with her relatives. I was on my own for a short while, but I could not afford the rent. A friend from home was looking for accommodation so I said she could move in, but eventually I moved out as she was inviting her boyfriend to stay overnight several times a week, and I really didn't need to be listening to them it was so embarrassing for me they carried on as if I was not there, there was no consideration for me. I said one day to her, you had all day to do your worst why wait until night time, so I told the landlord I was leaving, fixed up my rent and left it to her and her boyfriend. I moved in with my nursing friends whom I got to know through sport. They lived in a house with an adjoining shop, I remember one time after finishing my night duty, which was two weeks on and a week off, I went to bed at 8.30 a.m. and asked the girls to call me later around 3 o'clock. Everyone forgot and one of the girls called me at 8.15 p.m., I was so tired, I said, "Sure I'm only after going to bed." She said it's 8.15 p.m. your boyfriend is downstairs. I has slept for twelve hours with all the noise of the busy shop, and never heard a thing. The girls organized my 21st birthday in that house, cake, finger food nice background music, and then later we all went off to Mcgowan's pub for some live music.

Later that year the girls and I moved into a lovely big house on the new Cabra Road. I lived there with them, six of us until I got married, we had great times in that house, had many parties all civilized of course. We all got on very well and respected each other's privacy and space. The landlord was very happy with us as tenants, he said the house was kept immaculate, we cut the grass in the garden, etc. Then eventually one person moved out to get married, we thought he would increase our rent, no, there was no increase, even when a second person moved to the country to get married, still no increase in the rent. I was next to go to get married, then there were three. All that time the rent never increased as the landlord was happy with us as tenants. When I went the remaining girls moved to a smaller house until they all got married.

My boyfriend and I started to plan our wedding a year in advance. I asked the matron in early January that year just after Christmas as I thought I might get a better reception when the

Christmas rush was over. I made an appointment and was invited into her office. She was an elegant lady, wearing a black leather jacket, sitting behind the desk and to my surprise she was smoking a cigarette, and by the look of the ashtray on the table it wasn't her first one that morning, but she was the matron and the boss. I suppose it was normal at the time to smoke in the workplace, even though I never smoked. I asked her politely if I could have two weeks off in September to get married. She said, "Nurse Mc Guinness, students don't get holidays in September, and for all she knew the hospital could be closed by then," little did she know it would take another forty-odd years to close, I said to her I had to know as hotels were hard to come by, and it would take a few months to get letters of freedom from home as we were getting married in Dublin

Eventually she asked the nurses in the office if anyone might be retiring by then, they said possibly and she agreed to give me the time off. She always had two nurses to do the office work, rosters, etc. We decided on the Clare Manor Hotel near Artane. We used to have our dinner dances there, it was the best price we could get, and could barely afford it as we had put a deposit on a house in Swords Co. Dublin where we still live. I was good at sewing and made my wedding dress and the bridesmaids' dresses too. We invited 120 guests, most were our friends from the hospital and the many aunts and uncles my mother insisted on. I knew the aunties and uncles wouldn't travel to Dublin as that was a hassle in the day, so we ended up with ninety-six guests. We got engaged three months before our wedding, I hated long engagements, there were so many people in the hospital engaged for years and nothing happening, and I mean even up to ten years or more. I designed my own engagement ring and had it made in Appleby's in town, one of the nurses had a contact there.

We had to put the deposit on our house in June 1975, it was the end house on the road, I thought, *great, my boyfriend was to go by bus to Swords on a Saturday morning after his night duty which finished at 8 a.m., he had to be there before 1 p.m.* I was on duty in the alcoholic unit on the north circular road, I told the charge nurse who was a friend of ours, and I kept saying to him, I hope he gets there in time. He said of course he will, no one could miss something as important as that, but no he went to bed intending to get up at 11 but didn't hear his alarm and missed the deadline of 1 o'clock, he got there at two but the end house was gone. I was so disappointed, we went out to Swords on Monday and got a house in the middle of the road, the one we are still in, it was the most expensive sleep he ever had.

My boyfriend's brother was a priest, Father Michael as his mother used to call him, we just called him Mickey, and so he would do the ceremony for free in Rathmines Church. At that time, it was customary for girls to be married in their hometown, but we got married in Rathmines. Mickey had started the Rathmines gospel choir when the parish priest was away on leave, and boy was it a success and still is, unfortunately Mickey died of cancer when he was only fifty-four, at his last assignment to Cappamore as parish priest. He was the nicest priest I have ever known. He looked after all the family weddings, funerals and get-togethers. Years later he would say mass in the family home for us and our children. His sermons were simple but very relevant, and the crowds increased in Rathmines with the choir becoming famous.

We had our wedding there on the 14th of September 1976 it was a Tuesday. My husband was not a great planner and had to get the day worked for our wedding as he booked his holidays late, so on the Sunday night he still had not found anyone to work the day. So I just said I'll see you there at the church. That morning I had an appointment to get my hair done in Peter Marks, in town, my friend Anna made it for me, I was just going to do it myself but she insisted. We got the bus into town, got the hair done and again she insisted we get a taxi back the day that was in it.

My mum and dad arrived to the house in Cabra, the girls insisted I had a limousine to go to the church, personally I thought this was madness, anyway, we got one. So my dad and I travelled in the limousine to the church. We got married in Rathmines church with Billy's brother Mickey who was the priest there at that time and did the honours. After my dad walked me up the aisle, and he gave me away to Billy, we exchanged our vows and got married, he really approved of Billy, and probably thought to himself that's another one sorted, as one of my sisters had her wedding three months earlier. The gospel choir started up, played at our wedding, the music was breathtaking, we were so blessed to have such wonderful music and such a lovely church, the choir is still going strong to this day.

We had a lovely day in the Clare Manor Hotel, we booked a bus for the friends from the hospital as very few people had cars then. Billy had booked one of his friends the Buzzer to play the music at the wedding, and as things go he was late, but eventually the music was great for the rest of the night. We left to go on our honeymoon as was again customary, we hadn't booked into the hotel, nor did anyone else, but apparently the music went on late and everyone had a great time. We were stupid not to stay as we missed a lot of craic, everyone said the night was great, how customs have changed for the better. We got a taxi to our house in Swords which only had a bed, a cooker, and two stools in it, and spent our wedding night there, it wasn't the most glamorous of places, but it was our night and a great night.

The next morning we got the bus to the train station, as our honeymoon was a trip around Ireland on the train, stopping to the many friends who invited us to call on route. One of our friend's dad lived in Galway, and when we called to say hello, he had organized a great music session for us, and his parents insisted we take their bedroom as the honeymoon couple, I thought it was the nicest thing anyone could do. We said our goodbyes to everyone the next morning after a slap-up feed of a full Irish breakfast, and off on the train again. We did stay in some nice bed and breakfasts on our tour. This might seem simple now but it's all we could afford, at least we had our house. We spent a week traveling around and got back to reality.

We moved into our house, put sheets on the windows for curtains, people might laugh at that now, wedding presents were usually a pair of sheets, or a kettle etc., the biggest present we got was a super ser heater, which all of the girls I lived with bought together. The interest rates on mortgages at that time was seventeen and a half percent, so it took all of my wages and half of my husband's wages to pay the mortgage, so it was stay at home every night. We were back about a month when I was sick every day, I thought it was food poisoning I might have picked up on our travels, went to the doctor only to discover I was pregnant, pregnancy tests kits were not available then, oh my god, I was sick morning, noon and night, I couldn't go to work, the doctor put me on tablets to keep me from getting sick. I was reluctant to take them but he said otherwise it would be hospital on a drip.

I took a tablet each day but it made no difference so I stopped taking them, I was at home for a month just lying around and lost two and a half stone. I had to get back to work or all my sick leave entitlement would be gone. I was still sick but just had water, toast and scrambled eggs.

The nursing establishment thought I had anorexia, so I was called to the matron's office she said you have been off sick for weeks now, and you've lost so much weight, so I had to tell her I was pregnant. She looked at me and said, "You were quick off the mark there," I felt like telling her we threw caution to the wind now that we were married and had a place to live, but I just said I'm fine now it's just morning sickness, not that it was any of her business, you would think I was a child. I was in the admission Unit 10A and the charge there was very sympathetic and was determined to find something I could eat, she got me chips and coke from the canteen, which amazingly stayed down, so that was my diet for four months even though I was still sick until lunchtime every day. Travelling in on the bus was tough, I used to carry six plastic bags with me, I never made the journey without being sick so we used to go on the top deck not to annoy anyone, once I got over those few months I was fine and started gaining weight.

My friends and colleagues were very supportive of fellow nurses who were pregnant as there were no health and safety policies in place, so other nurses would do the heavy lifting of patients, again there was no training provided for this, so most nurses in my age bracket have had back operations as a result. The maternity leave was twelve weeks at that time so if you were overdue you had less time off afterwards, you were allowed to take a month's unpaid leave if you could afford it, so nurses often gave the wrong dates of when they were due, so they were able to work longer beforehand.

My first baby was five days overdue, a friend of ours, a nurse who lived in our estate gave us a lift to St James Hospital on a Monday. On Wednesday morning Dr Hanratty came around and said I would have to have an anaesthetic and go to the theatre as I had been in constant labour and nothing was happening. I said fine and signed on the dotted line. I woke up from the anaesthetic at six o'clock and asked where my baby was. The nurses said he was in the intensive care unit due to the difficult and lengthy labour and birth, but he was fine, it was just a precaution. I was not allowed out of bed as I was too weak. My husband and his brother Mickey the priest saw him before I did. I went to hospital on Monday in labour and he was born on Wednesday at four thirty, just in time for payday, I never saw my cheque that fortnight as my husband and friends had great celebrations.

I was still awake at midnight and this older nurse said to me to get some rest. I said to her I had my first baby at 4 o'clock today and I could not go to sleep until I could see him. She agreed to get me a wheelchair and wheeled me to the intensive care unit. She said you have to walk in, splash your face with water so I did. The nurses there showed me Mark, he was a beautiful little blonde-haired boy and looked so healthy. They asked me if I wanted to hold him, I just stroked him and said I could not, that I was afraid I might drop him, I knew I was going to faint. I woke up in bed and the older nurse was giving out saying she could get into trouble, I said to her it was worth it now I could sleep happily. I pointed to all the flowers, and told her to take any bouquet she wanted with her in the morning when she was finished her shift.

My husband's friend John promised me that if I ever had a baby he would bring me a bunch of yellow irises and low and behold he arrived in the maternity unit carrying them behind his back, it was sweet. We were in the hospital for six days after delivery, then we brought our beautiful son Mark home. In those times there were no husbands allowed into the labour ward, they just had to wait outside until the nurse would go out to them and give them the news. A lot of them including my husband spent time in the pub across the road from St James's checking from time to time for news. It was a lonely time for us and you would be lucky to get a nice nurse to give you support until you were ready to deliver your baby. The midwives were great and usually had more experience than junior doctors.

I remember when we got home, with little in the house, but we had a cradle and some of the usual baby stuff, I suddenly thought we have this new little person, it's not just us anymore. We were afraid to leave him on his own for a second, my husband had a few days off, and so when he went back to work I was alone with this little mite at my beck and call. I could hardly use the loo without taking him and his basket in with me. It was a very long day my husband left for work at 6.30 a.m. and only got home at 10 p.m. We worked a day on day off system so at least he was off every second day. I breastfed for a few weeks, but was exhausted, so I decided to bottle feed then. We had no fridge, so that was an absolute must for Mark's bottles, so thank god for the credit union, we got a loan and got the fridge, anything electrical was so expensive those days.

Time passed quickly and my maternity leave was up, I had to take a month's sick leave as I got an infection and was unfit to go back to work. Then I had to go back, my husband was not relishing the thought of minding an eight-week-old baby from 6.30. a.m. until 10 p.m., 9 p.m, if I could get a lift home. I remember the first night I came home the house was in disarray, cotton wool everywhere it was like a surgery, I laughed and asked him how many changes the child had he said 7. Mark was asleep due to have his next feed at 11 p.m. and my husband was ready to go out for a well-deserved pint. I was glad to get back to work, even though I loved my time at home twelve hours minding a tiny baby in a new estate was no joke, I had to get to know my neighbours.

Back to work and into the thick of things I was sent back to the geriatric wards, I enjoyed my time there but it was the same routine every day, wash, dress and feed the patients. We did do different things with the patients who were able to partake in activities, like helping them knit and sew, getting the paper for anyone who could read it having nice music in the ward and one antiquated TV on in the day room, we tried to make their day as enjoyable as possible. We got to know a lot of patients moving from ward to ward I was mostly in the geriatric wards then and some of the old characters would make you sad as they often had no visitors and again some had who did visit regularly, but they were few and far between. They all had their own little habits and it was their way or no way.

Then when Mark was thirteen months old I was pregnant again, I had the usual awful sickness, hyperemesis gravidarum, and had to go off work for six weeks, I got my husband to cook marks food the previous day as I just managed to feed him, the smell of food made me retch. After the six weeks, it was back to work in the geriatric wards which was not great for anyone's back let alone mine, but the girls were good as usual and would not allow me to do any heavy lifting, I would give out the medicines and do paperwork. Our paperwork was limited at that time and was written in the nurses' notes, it was the best place to look if you wanted information about the patient, the rest of the chart was used for the doctor's notes, which in some cases was illegible. There were no occupational therapists, psychotherapists, or physiotherapists in the services at that time, the nurses did all that, occupying patients in things they enjoyed, and patients who were not confined to bed for particular reasons were walked regularly, accompanied to the toilet a couple of times a day, we never used catheters which could be a source of infection, and patients sitting all day in chairs were in danger of getting pressure sores, which we always prevented.

I worked as long as I could during my second pregnancy, as usual, I had severe morning, noon, and night sickness for the first three months, even after that I would be fine going to work but as soon as I would get there my blood pressure would drop, I would grab a pot of tea and go to the office, lie on the floor legs elevated and drink the pot of tea in about twenty

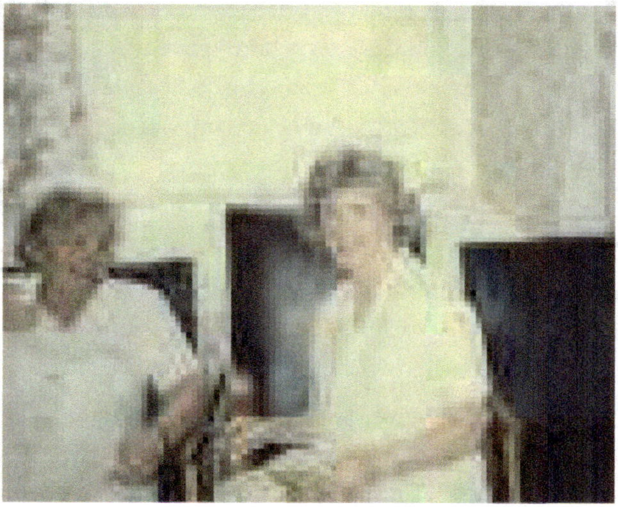

minutes, then I would be fine again, it became a joke when I would come in the door the charge nurse would hand me the pot of tea saying "See you in twenty minutes." This picture is of a lovely senior nurse Myra and I, having a cuppa in the dayroom of unit D. I was grand after the three to four months of sickness passed, I spent that pregnancy in unit D, I was due in three weeks and feeling great, the girls kept saying to me to stay on another week or two, I felt that might be pushing it so I went on maternity leave on a Friday, and Fiona was born on a Monday, three days later, she arrived three weeks early, and another eighteen hour labour. I had a haemorrhage afterwards and was given a few units of blood, which years later I discovered I was in the category of people who had to be tested for the hepatitis C scandal, I was fine thank god.

That night she was born I could hear her crying but they would not let me out of bed. I asked if would somebody just feed her, she had a big mop of red hair, eventually someone fed her. I got home after five days, and life was hectic with two small babies. I had to gain weight again. I loved my time off especially as Fiona arrived early and gave me extra time at home. At that time maternity leave was twelve weeks, six weeks before your due date and six weeks afterwards, so we all had to fiddle with our due dates. Six weeks later we had the christening as we had with Mark, that was the custom at that time, and the grannies and grandads and relatives arrived. Billy's brother Mickey did the ceremony as usual, it was great having our own lovely priest. We just had a celebration at home as most people did then with a buffet etc., it was lovely.

Soon I was back to work again in the geriatric wards, I was assigned to Unit D again, in the lower house, most of the patients had not changed in the two months I was off on maternity leave, once patients were placed in a unit they rarely went anywhere else, unless they passed away.

I was transferred to another geriatric unit after my next holidays, the charge in this unit was not very pleasant to the patients or us. She lived in the nurses' home and perhaps the reason was because she did not have many interests outside work, this was common for quite a few people whose work was their life. Lots of the grannies in this unit had very bad swallow, and even with their food mashed up, still found it difficult to eat. I was back with her one evening at teatime, I was feeding three grannies at a time to give them a chance to swallow their food three chairs in front of me, the charge was feeding another lady who had trouble swallowing, she got annoyed with her and was just going to slap her across the face when I jumped up, and caught her arm. I said if you do that I will go straight over to the matron's office and report you. She grunted and said you feed her then, and I did. I eventually persuaded her to get a blender to avoid any other instances, as

I found it very useful at home for my son when he was small, if there was a lump of anything in his food it would all come back up. This blended food worked very well and dinners tasted great, at least the grannies were getting their nourishment. I just kept out of her way while I was on duty there.

We had some craic with the students. If a new student started in the unit we would have the craic with them, as many staff nurses had with us in the past. One evening when the laundry was delivered to the ward which we had to count, as if we would run off with the grannies' knickers or nightdresses, I said to the student she had to iron the grannies knickers. She looked at me with disbelief, I was joking of course. I went off to get an ironing board and told her I would be back shortly, just stack up the forty knickers and she would be done in no time. When I got back she had them ready, I said I'm only joking, thank god she said I don't iron anything, a bit of laughter made the work lighter and bonded people together.

It was in this unit that I got septicaemia, I got a cut on my hand one morning, as the day went on it was throbbing and the pain was dreadful. I showed it to the ward sister, she said she would dress it for me with a Kaylene poultice, she put it on, but by late afternoon it was really painful. I phoned a friend who said he would be off early at 7.30. p.m. and we would make the doctor's by 8. Unfortunately the ward sister would not let me off, so I had to get the bus and missed the doctors. When I went home I put another poultice on it and went to bed, my husband was working the next day he was gone at 7 a.m., I didn't sleep much that night, took more painkillers throughout the night. At 9 a.m. I had to ring the doctor I was in agony, I couldn't go to the surgery as I had two small children and no car, he came to our house, when he took off the dressing he seemed alarmed, my little finger was totally green and swollen.

He said he would have to lance it and drain the infection, I said go ahead, the pain was so bad and my arm was getting stiff. He cut my finger drained it and dressed it, then gave me an intramuscular injection of antibiotics and some vials for my husband to give me for the next few days, he knew we were nurses, then continued with oral antibiotics for two weeks. He said I was a very lucky lady that morning that I had called him, any later and I would be an ambulance job or worse. I was off work for three weeks, as it took that long to clear the infection. The doctor must have put septicaemia on the certs, because when I returned for duty I was told I would not be working in the geriatric wards again, I said fine, but all of this could have been avoided if the ward sister had let me off to go to the doctor's. It wasn't mentioned again, if it happened today they might be facing a legal case for negligence, she never even apologized or asked how I was.

So I was assigned to the upper house in one of the admission units, 10A. It was a very busy unit with young and older people admitted for acute reasons, and there were also several patients there for years as there was nowhere else to transfer them to. It was such a mix, with a large dormitory for twenty-five people and another day room cum-dormitory for ten people who had no liberty or had to be observed closely. It was dreadful trying to look after these supposedly ten people, that might have been reasonable, but there would be up to ten more people sent down to us for the day to look after as well. Anyone that looked crooked at the charge nurse on our shift she would send them to us in the observation ward which was very small and had ten beds in it.

This unit was also one of the units where initially ECT (electric compulsive therapy) was performed in the hospital six days a week, Monday, Wednesday, and Friday, in 10 A, and Tuesday, Thursday, and Saturday in unit O. The beds were all set up in the upper dormitory, and an anaesthetist would come to give the sedation and muscle relaxant to the patients who were receiving this treatment. The muscle relaxant made a huge difference to patients receiving ECT, prior to that in the past there were several reports of patients having injuries when having straight ECT, like fractures due to the intensity of the seizure.

I was asked to assist with the ECT on those days, I was glad to have a break from the observation ward as the noise levels were so high you could hardly hear yourself talk. There was one lady there who had severe intellectual disability and when she let fly, she let fly. She was so strong, she would fling tables and chairs and anything she could lay her hands on, at anyone that got in her way, I witnessed this so many times and had to help sedate her, and try and protect the other patients who were terrified of her. One of the senior nurses was great at reading the signs and before she got the chance to explode and get violent, she would say to me get her medication, she was prescribed PRN medication that is a dose of urgent medication if she needed it other than her regular doses.

This senior nurse was very used to her and knew what amount of largactil she needed. We had peace for the day then, again she had no plan for placement, her parents could not look after her, and so she was what was called a long-term care patient. Much later in the eighties, she was transferred to St. Ita's Intellectual Disability services which is where her needs could be met. The first time I saw ECT in unit 10 A, which was on Monday, I thought it was unusual and some might say frightening and some doctors did not agree with it as a treatment refusing to partake in it, they said they had a conscientious objection to ECT. The patient would be given a short acting anaesthetic and muscle relaxant, and electrodes placed on both temples, given a shock and subsequently have a fit, then return to normal.

Some patients would not remember it and would be prescribed three sessions initially, and more if there was no improvement in their condition. This treatment was used for mania and depression, not for acute depression but for endogenous depression, where antidepressant medications did not work, and I can honestly say that it did work very well for many people. I remember one lady who had three ECT treatments and did not need it again for ten years. There was a man in the male wards who was so depressed he would not eat, and after a few treatments, he was well again. Some patients who were totally resistant to any medications might eventually have to have a maintenance dose of ECT every two weeks or longer depending on their condition.

After my next holidays, I was assigned to a long-stay unit 9 where again patients had mixed diagnoses. Some of the patients were able to attend an occupational therapy unit where there was printing, craftwork and where the patients also did packaging for various firms. They were occupied off the units and given a small wage for their work, they would have an exhibition of their work once a year. The beautiful picture of the swan shown earlier in the book was done by one of the ladies in unit 9. She was a beautiful younger girl, not like the other patients, she was gentle and kind, I never remember any relatives coming to see her.

There were a lot of violent patients in this unit and not many staff, I remember coming on duty early and the charge nurse having to deal with a very violent lady, she said to me as soon as I arrived, go to the medicine cupboard and get the prescribed medication by injection for this lady, I did hurriedly while she tried to calm the patient whom there was no talking to and eventually we managed to sedate her between us. Some of these patients had visitors, but not very many, another lady who got married young ended up in this unit she had schizophrenia, apparently it only appeared a year or two after she got married. Her husband used to visit her every two weeks, bring her cigarettes and fruit, it was sad, she didn't realize he was her husband, and he visited for many years.

Another lady in this unit became pregnant while out on pass (a day's leave or sometimes overnight). We all wondered what would happen. Miraculously she had the baby, and with her son to focus on, with the help of her mother, she was discharged. A few years later while I was on duty there again she visited with her son, he was about five and seemed happy, she was coping very well, with regular review at a psychiatric outpatient clinic, community nurse visits, social services, and community supports.

My next unit was 1C it was the top floor of a three-storey building with stone steps to every floor, there were forty patients in this unit. Most of these patients were able to look after themselves as regards dressing and eating. They were all supervised by the nurses while bathing as was the custom at that time. There were some violent patients in this unit too, we would be sent off on the grounds near the football pitch for an hour in the morning weather permitting, and an hour and a half in the afternoon. This was very good for the patients, they loved getting out into the fresh air, though it was a job for us to keep an eye on all of them. The male patients in the units underneath would be out too, and often nature being nature, they were attracted to each other. My husband told me that they used to be sent out in the evenings on sex watch to check the grounds for patient liaisons. I did see a couple at a later date from a different unit I worked in on my way back from tea break, I just asked her if she was coming in, and she told me in a while, so I left them at it, she said it was great, she was on a contraceptive injection, so we didn't have to worry about pregnancy.

In this block, 1A, 1B, 1C, there was a communal dining room for the men and women from these three wards, with long tables set in the dining room. It was difficult to keep the men and women apart, they often wandered to each other's tables asking for a fag, or sometimes they liked the look of someone. When they were all seated, we would serve the soup, dinner, and desert, then tea, it was bedlam, and they were very impatient. Some like children with no patience, and you had to be very strict with them. Scuffles often broke out and some patients were removed back to the unit and their lunch would be brought up to them on a tray by staff.

On one such occasion I was asked to bring dinner up to one of these ladies, and just as I entered the unit and was about to put the dinner on the table for her, the other nurse who was in the unit said, "Quick she's behind you," I ducked and she missed me, the dinner went all over the place, she was very elated, but this lady was wicked, she intended to injure me, the violent wild look in her eyes said it all. I never minded any patient who was genuinely ill and elated, and not vindictive which she was. I managed to back away slowly as far as the office and squeezed in the door, the other nurse phoned for help, one of the male nurses from downstairs came to our assistance and we managed to sedate her. This lady used to have these outbursts regularly but she particularly attacked any nurse who was on their own with her.

We had to have a policy put in place that no nurse would be alone with her, she had already injured too many nurses, my friend was unlucky and had lumps of her hair pulled out and was thumped in the face and body, she was black and blue, and in pain. She was off sick for a few weeks, the powers that be thought this was part of the job, so nurses had to find ways to protect themselves. Every nurse wanted to work in safety and get home to their families and children at the end of the day. No nurse should expect to be assaulted, but it did happen regularly, as some violent patients were not placed appropriately, there were not enough secure units where staffing ratios would be increased.

There were no counselling services for nurses who were attacked by patients, you were just expected to get on with it, and your medical expenses were not even reimbursed.

During the eighties there was a management decision to mix some of the wards to have male and female patients together, there was the notion that it would be a more natural environment, and patients would communicate with each other. Firstly mixing of male and female nurses, and integrating male and female patients was started in The Operant unit where male and female patients and staff were mixed, this unit was also called the token economy unit and was run by one of our consultants, the idea of training patients towards positive behaviour by earning their entitlements. They were to engage in programmes and got tokens for their food, day passes outings etc.

Some of these patients were not able to access these programmes so would not have enough tokens for their dinner, however, we nurses could not deprive any patient of food whatever about outings, etc. so we would just give it to them anyway, we just didn't inform the consultant. The sleeping arrangements were a large dormitory divided into two sides male and female, which was probably difficult for the night staff to monitor, they had to sit in the dormitory at the doors to ensure no hanky panky went on. The consultant was reviewing the patients one day with me, and after interviewing Sarah he said to me she's a washout. I said I thoroughly agree, she never takes part in anything she's not really fit for this unit, I thought he had given up trying to rehabilitate her.

He said no I mean she needs a washout of all her medication and start again. I said to him she is very chronic you might need to send her to a more secure unit to do that she is barely civil with all her medication, so he agreed, he tried in vain it was not long before she was back and as chronic as ever, I said to him you tried you can't cure them all. We had some great times in this unit, one day one of the male nurses who could imitate anyone's voice answered the phone saying, "Hello this is the operant unit Dr F speaking," he didn't realize it was Dr F. We were all waiting for his daily visit, when he came in, he was livid took the nurse aside and advised him never to do that again. This consultant was very interested in the homeless and helping patients to live in community settings, he opened a hostel in Rathmines, a day centre in Ushers Quay, two hostels in the inner city, and lastly a large hostel in Howth Co Dublin, which was staffed by nurses and auxiliary staff. He was always so diligent about his work and unlike most consultants his writing was impeccable.

One of the other geriatric units I worked in was 10B, there were thirty patients in this unit twenty males and ten females, obviously the sleeping quarters were separate but the day rooms were mixed. The ladies liked to keep to themselves, and very few mixed with the older men who had dementia and various other diagnoses, and could be aggressive towards them, and some of the men had filthy habits, spitting on the floor, dreadful language etc. This was a mixed staffing ward, we all got on well together, the morning rush of getting patients up, washed, fed, and medication usually went well. I would always be asked to do the medications with the charge nurse, I knew the patients' medications off by heart, not many prescriptions changed unless a patient was on antibiotics or medications were reviewed because of relapse. We would split the bathing list we did the ladies the male nurses did the men.

Sometimes we would give the lads a dig out and bathe some of the men. My friend Anna and I were finished the ladies one morning, so we decided to see who was on the men's list, so we went off with Paddy for his bath. I said to Anna he looks very clean, but he's on the list, this poor man could not speak and just as we were finished and had him looking fresh and smart one of the male nurses said, "Where are you going with him?" We said we just gave him a bath, the male nurse said well so did we, we just laughed and said, "He's sparkling so." The charge nurse asked me to help with the shaving which I did, some of the men were grumpy and would move their faces while I was trying to shave them resulting in a little nick on their faces. I was not used to shaving men. The charge would say to me I can see you did the shaving, I asked, "How do you know?"

He said, "I can see the trail of blood, but keep practicing you will get better." We had some great times in this unit, some of the ladies would give us their shopping list for their little treats, they had no visitors, so we would get their shopping on our breaks, and they would be waiting for us to return from lunch or tea.

Management also decided to mix some male and female staff in more units, the male admission unit with thirty patients. It was different nursing the men who had a lot of disgusting habits, and most of them were not very hygienic. However they actually improved with the female input, and so did the decor of the units, a woman's touch. Some of the male nurses were reluctant to work with us at first, but they soon got used to the females, and made the day more interesting. The admission unit was so different from the geriatric unit, you never knew from day to day who would be admitted with acute symptoms needing close observation and treatment. There were also some patients who were there for a long time as there were no places to move them to once their acute illness was stable. I remember Christy so well, he was a lovely man, he had been a grade sergeant who suffered from depression when he retired and eventually ended up in 3A. I asked him one morning if he would like a bath as he was so scruffy he wasn't too keen, he looked at me with disbelief. I said to him gently, "Don't worry, I am used to bathing men, don't be embarrassed."

"I'm not," he said. He probably thought I looked like a child but the uniform helped. So we got on great and he would ask me for his bath when I was on duty there, he actually started talking about his life in the guards and how hard it was. He never got married, so had no children just one or two siblings who never visited him. I thought, *this is so sad, you spend your life serving the public and you end up here,* at least he was content and safe. My husband and other male nurses used to bring in clothes for the patients. I went home one night and my husband said to me, "You know I saw a lad walking up the grounds yesterday and he was wearing a check jacket just like mine."

I said that was yours, I used to send in his clothes with my friend, if I gave him a bag to bring in he would arrive home with most of them, saying I like that jumper or trousers.

This male admission unit was so overcrowded there could be thirty-five to thirty-six patients for thirty beds, so my first job every morning was to phone the long-stay wards and see if they had a vacancy to lodge a stable patient overnight. I would have to get at least six to seven every night, this was very stressful on the patients, having to move to a different ward every night, lodging out as it was called. Eventually with staff and union intervention where nurses were instructed not to cooperate with lodging out of any patient, management decided to open a twelve bedded prefab unit to cater for the overflow of patients. This took a lot of work selecting the best and most stable of patients in the unit to sleep there at night and return in the morning to the admission unit. It was of course, the nurses who knew the patients well and recommended them to the doctors who had to daily sign their transfer. Some junior doctors would hardly know the patients as most of them were on a six monthly rotation placement. It was a temporary solution with one nurse on night duty, but when the patients returned each morning the unit was totally overcrowded again. This situation continued until the hospital was downsizing, and beds were reduced. An ECT suite was installed in the male admission with a dedicated nurse there for the ECT sessions, rather than having ECT on some of the units, which was a great improvement, and patients had time to recover and not interfere with ward routines in the other units.

There were some units like the block, the highly secure units, 8A and 8B, O and R, where it was too dangerous to mix the staff and patients.

My husband worked as charge nurse in 8B in later years and was telling me that one day a particular patient who had attacked nurses in another hospital was being transferred there as they could not manage him. He arrived escorted by six Gardaí in handcuffs, my husband opened the door and told the Gardaí they could remove the handcuffs, then he called a senior nurse and asked him to take care of the patient who was still shouting and violent. The nurse said to him, "You are now in St Brendan's, we do not tolerate that sort of behaviour here do you understand me, because when the shit hits the fan here it hits the fan, do you want me to elaborate?"

"No," said the patient.

"So now like a good lad we are going into a single room until your doctor gets here it's for your own good."

"Ok, ok," said the patient and went quietly into the room with the nurse, the doctor subsequently arrived.

Another day a very eloquent consultant was interviewing a young patient with my husband present. She asked him if there was anything troubling him or anything on his mind he wanted to discuss. The patient replied, "The only thing on my mind at this present moment is spending the night with you." My husband said we will terminate this interview for now and do it later, when the patient was escorted out of the office he said to the consultant, "These young lads get very excited when they see a lady in a skirt so trousers might be better for these interviews."

She laughed and said, "I'll remember that." There are so many other stories that other nurses have that would be very enlightening.

St. Brendan's was the regional unit for very disturbed patients, there were seclusion rooms or padded cells where patients spent time out when they were a danger to themselves and others. They had to be monitored closely, two or three staff would go into the room to check their observations and general well-being, empty the piddle pot, change their clothes or straight jacket if it was soiled, and give them their meals and medications. If they were too unwell and refused their medication, they would have to get it intramuscularly by injection, which again could be difficult. Most patients would settle after a couple of days, or even hours sometimes. Some of these patients were very violent and many nurses got injured and retired from work as a result of their injuries.

I was working in Unit O when the first cameras were installed inside the entrance door to the seclusion rooms, the camera was placed very high up near the roof so the patient could not get at it. I was in the office observing the three rooms, in two rooms, I could see the patients on their beds, but in the other one, I could not see the patient at all. This was Maria's room, she was screaming and shouting and banging the door so viciously that the camera fell down and she was holding it. I went to her room and asked her to calm down and we would open the door, we asked her to move away from the door, she said she would. We opened the door carefully and the camera was hurled past us, we had to close the door again and wait for her to calm down. She eventually did, took her medications, and we let her out in a few hours. She was a likable but devious character, she was mildly mentally handicapped and difficult to reason with, all part of the job, she eventually was sent to the intellectual disability services in St Ita's.

Another evening, a patient smashed crockery in the dining room, I cut my hand trying to retrieve the plate. I had to go to the Richmond Hospital casualty, I had my hand bandaged by another nurse and was instructed by the deputy matron to go and get it seen to. So I walked through the grounds, through the gate to the Richmond, into casualty, I got four stitches in my hand and an anti-tetanus and returned to the ward luckily it was nearly eight o'clock, wrote my incident report, and I got home at 9:30 p.m., back to work as usually next day on, no time off given. These secure units were intense units to work in. I spent quite a few rostered times in Unit O, while other nurses spent a lot of time in Unit R, which was probably more volatile. On one occasion, I worked in Unit R when one of the patients who went missing was found three months later. She had drowned after walking into the sea, the Gardaí came to the unit to ask if someone on the staff could identify her, the charge in the unit said she would go, the Gardaí said it might not be possible to identify her as she was in the sea for so long, the only thing the nurse recognized were her runners. She always wore specific colourful ones. The Gardaí thanked her and said they would do DNA test if any relatives were found to let them know. I could see the charge nurse was pretty shaken up by the experience, she wasn't expecting it to be so gruesome, and we all gave her our support.

A few years later, when I was acting Assistant Director on night duty, as a panel of deputies and charges nurses did on a rotational basis, a lady was very violent in Unit O, and the nurses were trying to hold this strong lady down on the bed to sedate her, in the scuffle the junior nurse accidentally gave the sedation to another nurse instead of the patient, I arrived on the scene and had to call an ambulance for the nurse as we did not know how she would react, then we had to reorganize to safely give the patient the sedation. The nurse was fine, she was monitored in the Mater Hospital and slept for two days. That is why training in ways to do things safely is so important. Now, there is regular training for all staff TMVA-Therapeutic management of violence and aggression, the trainers do regular refresher courses to keep up to date.

In one of the geriatric units where my husband was working, he came back after his tea one evening, and the female nurse working there asked him to come quickly. One patient called Timmy had taken a turn, this man had not spoken in over ten years, and he had dementia. When my husband took his hand he sat up in the bed and thanked him and all the staff for looking after him. He said he could see his brother on the other side and was going to meet him now. He spoke very clearly, he said to my husband, "Don't bother phoning for a doctor, I'm going now," and then he lay down and passed away peacefully with a smile on his face. My husband and nurse Eileen couldn't believe it, they were amazed. This is just an example of true events that happened and I'm sure many of my colleagues have many more memories and stories they witnessed. Another memory again from my husband, who was telling me that the consultant was doing his reviews of some of the patients. This morning, he was reviewing Tom, who had a habit of barking in the middle of a conversation, which happened in conversation with the consultant. My husband passed no heed as all the male staff were used to it. The consultant said to my husband, "This is most unusual."

He asked Tom, "Why are you barking?"

Tom replied, "Because I have a dog in my throat."

"How long is he there?" asked the consultant.

"Since he was a pup, of course," replied Tom. My husband said to the consultant, who was new in the hospital, "It's a firm fixed belief he has, but it does not cause him any distress. Others have tried to treat him but no one has succeeded, so he just gets on with his day with the odd bark or several. Another unusual patient we all knew was."

"The dummy" he was a man out and about most of the time unless he misbehaved, waved to everyone, or knew everyone, he could not speak. The only words he learned to speak was "fuck off" if anyone annoyed him. He was clever and knew how to get what he wanted. When the first mobile phone came, the Nokia, my friend got an upgrade and gave him her old one. He was chuffed, pretending to ring everyone, there was no credit in it but he could hear it ringing and had it up to his ear listening, full of his own importance.

We had two churches, the Catholic Church, and the Protestant Church, there were two masses in the Catholic Church every Sunday, 10 and 11 o'clock masses, and for all special occasions throughout the year. St Patrick's Day, Easter, Christmas, patients' funerals, etc. We had a lovely Chaplin, Fr Pierce O Doubhall. He could say mass in twenty mins with a nice sermon and it never seemed rushed. He was a character, very good to patients and staff. One of the male nurses used to serve at mass, one morning, the nurse said to Fr Pierce, "You know some patients are coming up for communion twice." He said he hadn't noticed but said the next time you see a patient coming twice, give me a tap on the elbow. Next the nurse serving mass wanted to play a trick on his fellow nurse who came up for communion. He tapped Fr Pierce on the elbow, Fr Pierce said to the nurse, who he thought was a patient, "You already got communion."

"I did not," the nurse said.

Fr Pierce said, "I'm not giving it to you again," the nurse waited and waited and eventually walked back to his seat in disgust. After mass, he went into the sacristy to confront Fr Pierce, who said, "I'm sorry, but your buddy here was playing a prank on you," he laughed it off. These sort of things happened, not regularly, of course.

There were only a few protestant and church of Ireland patients in the hospital, they had mass once a month, where a clergyman from their church would come in and say mass. This church was used at a later date by Dr Ivor Browne for halotropic sessions.

Having worked in most of the units around the hospital, I was eventually sent to the alcoholic unit. This unit was on the north circular road at the very north point of the grounds beyond the football grounds. This large house was originally the Registered Medical Superintendent (RMS), what a beautiful house he had to live in, on its own grounds with beautiful trees and shrubs. Years earlier, prior to it being an alcoholic unit and vacated by the RMSs, in 1967, some of the male nurses had to sleep there in the sitting room while awaiting accommodation, then three large houses on the north circular road became the male nurses' residences, they were later turned into high and medium support hostels and a day centre.

My boyfriend had a place in one of these houses sharing a double room, their linen was supplied from the hospital laundry as ours was in the nurses' home, and only most lads were not as particular as the ladies for changing their beds. The houses were lovely and all had front and back gardens. The lads used to hop over the wall to go to work, through the football pitches, and to their allotted wards. I called for my boyfriend one lunchtime on my day off, only to see one male nurse climbing over the wall. I think he was a bit under the weather from the night before and was heading for the canteen for a bit of dinner. I thought he would injure himself, he floated over the wall but when we followed, he was fine.

I worked in this unit for a few months, as I did not do night duty after we had our first baby, so I was there until my next holidays. This unit was an eye-opener for me. There were twenty-four beds, twelve male and twelve female. They were divided by a large staircase, with bedrooms and bathrooms on each side of the landing. There was a kitchen, a dining room, and a sitting room downstairs. There was also another room where an outpatient clinic was held weekly. At the back of the building, to the right were the staff rooms, changing room, and toilet. The people admitted here for detoxification and counselling services had to be alcohol-free, and want treatment, some were also addicted to gambling. They would spend four weeks in intensive therapy with counsellors from Stanhope Street, this was rough having to confront their addictions in group sessions. Every morning, we got a urine sample from the patients to test for any alcohol, drugs, etc.

One morning, I asked this young lady for a sample and normally, we would wait at the door for them, these patients were very cunning. I was called away for a moment and this lady managed to get an older lady to give a sample, saying she collected her bottle for her. When tested it, of course, it was negative, so I asked her for another sample and waited outside the toilet this time and sure enough, it was positive. There were plenty of ways for them to get someone to slip in a bottle, with some other person's sample, they were very clever.

This was a detached large house on its own grounds and often patients would go walking around the grounds in the evening. As it was a mixed group of people often, love affairs would emerge, you got to notice all of the little signs. After their four weeks of therapy, people were discharged and offered follow-on services in Stanhope Street for the patient, their relatives, and children, Al-Anon, Al-ateen, and Gamblers Anonymous. I had a strange incident one morning. This lady was looking for the morning-after pill following a liaison the night before, which she obviously thought was not a good idea in the broad light of day.

I was given the task by the consultant of ringing around all of the well-woman clinics in the area. I had no problem with that, my male colleague was in the office with me, it was a very small office and not very private, he kept looking strangely at me. I said, "It was urgent," eventually I got a clinic that the lady could attend in the afternoon, so I made the appointment for 2 p.m. He was bewildered and asked me if I wanted to swap lunch breaks. I said, "No you're fine."

He said, "What about the appointment?" He couldn't help overhearing and thought it was for me. I said no, "It's for the lovers," then he understood and laughed. She went to her appointment and was advised on contraception.

One of the saddest admissions we had was when a twelve-year-old boy arrived with his mother. She was in an awful state and very inebriated, she could hardly say her name, then she urinated on the floor. He started crying, I sat her down to be assessed for admission and brought him into our kitchen. I asked our housekeeper if she would make him tea and sandwiches, cake, etc. She was a lovely lady and empathized with his position. She couldn't believe how hungry he was and gave him loads to eat and did packed lunches for the kids at home. The doctor admitted his mother for detoxification and asked me to get some information from him. He had settled after his food, which he badly needed, so I asked him about the family, who was at home, and about his dad.

He said he was the eldest and had a brother, ten and two sisters, eight and six. He didn't know where his dad was and could not remember when he saw him last. He said he had to leave his brother minding his sisters when he came here with his mother. She asked him to bring her for treatment. I explained to him that they could not stay alone in the flat in Ballymun alone, we would have to get a relative, or if not, social services until his mother was well enough, and that could be quite a while. He started crying again, I told him he needed someone to look after him and his brother and sisters. There were no relatives, I think his mother had burnt all of those bridges of support. I told him social services would do their best to keep them together but it might not be possible.

I also told him he could call in a few days as his mother would be given medication and needed to sleep a lot, and I would be here for the next few weeks. He went off with the social worker to get sorted out. I asked her to let him visit his mother in a few days or a week. This was the last chance for the mother, and when she came around after detoxification, she agreed to attend the programme and turn her life around for herself and her four beautiful children. It didn't happen immediately but eventually she got there with support, aftercare for herself and her children.

Another admission was an eighteen-year-old girl. She was distraught but knew she needed treatment. She was very anxious but I managed to reassure her that this was the only way, she had tried herself and her family at home without success, she learned some hard lessons while she was there and she too made big changes to her life. We noticed her confidence and maturity grow every day. At the end of her treatment, she was discharged home with follow-up treatment for her and her family. Some people were successful and some were not and became repeat admissions, but it was very rewarding to see the success stories.

There was a man from Cavan admitted, he was about forty-six. I was asked to show him his shared room and introduce him to his fellow roommates. I gave him a list of the rules and his sheets to make up his bed, he said he never made his bed and would I make it.

I said, "You must be joking who makes your bed at home?" He told me his mother, who was in her late sixties, always made it. "Well," I just said to him, "it's ten a.m. now and you should have it made before the night staff come in at eight thirty if you want to sleep here." His jaw dropped but eventually he did it about 6 p.m.

I was in that unit for about three months, and as well as having inpatients and outpatient clinics, and people calling at 7 or 8 a.m. for Antabuse before going to work daily, there was a weekly AA (Alcoholics Anonymous) meeting, the meeting went very well with people who were discharged attending, and anyone else who found the time of seven p.m. useful if they were working. The consultant in this unit came in one Thursday morning complaining of shingles. He was in pain and said he would have to go home, I said to him, "If you are interested, I can get you the cure tomorrow. I will drive home to Ardee, my mother has an old lady in the bog who has it, and it works in three days." I said, "It stinks the first time you put it on, it's a paste mixed with holy water, but your pain will be gone on the first day."

I thought he would laugh but he said, "Please do, how much is it?"

I said, "You just give a donation, usually a fiver." He gave me ten euros. I went to Ardee the next morning and got the cure. I left it in the unit for him, marked it confidential as promised, told him to follow the instructions, he arrived at the unit Monday morning cured, he thanked me, he couldn't believe it. I said I got it for a lot of people in the hospital and it always worked. We should have analysed it and bottled it.

One particular evening in August, when such a meeting was about to start and a volunteer (former alcoholic) had set up the room, a patient who had recently been discharged had arrived. I was in the office and heard an altercation between the two men, I knew this meant trouble when I saw them take off their jackets and immediately picked up the phone to ring the guards. Unfortunately for me the discharged patient saw me ran into the office, pulled the phone off the desk and the line out of the socket, he then grabbed me and threw me on the stone floor. I could feel my neck and back twinge. I screamed as loud as I could. The secretary came in from next door, she normally would have been gone home by five, but she had filing to catch up on and I was giving her a lift home.

I told her to get the patients in the sitting room, the male patients who were looking at a football match, to go after him, and asked her to phone the guards. When the guards arrived, he was long gone. They asked me if I wanted to press charges, and if I was ok, I felt dazed and shocked. This man was fifteen stone and I was eight and a half stone at the time. I told the guards I knew who he was, but that it was unlikely he would get any sentence as he also had mental health problems, as well as being an alcoholic, so I never pressed any charges.

I phoned the Assistant Director of Nursing to tell him what had happened, he literally asked me to leave a special incident report on my way home to his office, he never even asked me if I was ok, did I need medical attention, or anything else? I was still in shock and went through the motions. When the night nurses came in, they asked if I was ok to drive home and phoned my husband. I said I would be ok as my friend the secretary, would be traveling halfway home with me. When she got out of the car, I just cried, to think I was after being physically assaulted and injured and no one in nursing management cared or even came to my assistance. I felt terrible to think we were left so exposed to danger in our working environment and no back up from the people in charge when we needed them. I said goodnight to my friend and drove all the way home crying. My husband was shocked when he saw me.

When I got home I was sore and bruised and my neck and back were killing me. I had a hot bath, took Panadol, and tried to sleep. The next day the doctor who was working in the unit phoned me at home and said I should get medical help. I went to my GP, who put me on sick leave, a great consultant who worked in the hospital and who we all respected referred me to a consultant in St Josephs in Raheny. He admitted me immediately as I needed traction for my neck. I was on this traction a few hours a day and anti-inflammatory drugs for three weeks. My husband had to take time off work, his holidays, to mind the children. When I got home, I was to continue on the anti-inflammatory drugs, which I only took at night time to get some sleep. I was off sick for three months, I could not lift my children, and I had to wear a collar during the day for support. I decided I had to stop taking these anti-inflammatories, so I only took one a night for the next week, then stopped them. That was in December, when I stopped taking them I was so sick I could not eat anything. I was sent to a gastroenterologist who did a scope and said I had the equivalent of third-degree burns in my intestinal tract. I did not realize the anti-inflammatories were burning my insides, and neither did the doctor. He put me on medication to help heal my intestinal system, and my diet was yogurts, custard, and ice cream for the next six weeks.

None of the medications worked and I ended up having a Nissans fundoplication operation in the Meath hospital which only worked for three months. So to this day I am left with ongoing medical problems and have had five surgeries all because of that incident at work. There was no compensation then, and you were also on basic wage when out on sick leave.

I was out sick for months and ended up on half pay, which was very difficult to cope with, as well as all the medical expenses, and not being able to care for your children. This patient was admitted to St Vincent's Hospital Fairview in future times. As a gesture of goodwill on the management's side so that he would not attack any nurse in St Brendan's again. A few years later he was admitted back to St Brendan's but thankfully not in any of the wards I was in, I saw him walking down to the assessment unit. I was in my car, I actually felt like confronting him but I knew there would be no point, he probably didn't even remember me and all the suffering he caused me and my family.

The assessment unit was another mixed unit, it had eight beds for males and females and male and female staff. I spent one or two, night duties there as well as day duty, one night on night duty a female patient was admitted. She was homeless and had mental health issues as well. The sister on night duty knew her well. She said to me she will go in the morning, she usually just stays the night and will go back to the streets. I noticed she had no shoes and she was filthy, her feet were all cut, I asked the sister if I could give her a bath? The sister said good luck with that, but I wanted to clean her up. I waited until the medication had taken the edge off her erratic, hostile mood, then brought a basin and every lotion and cream I could find.

She reluctantly agreed to a wash, a bath was out of the question, then I soaked her feet to soften them, and put antiseptic cream all over them. She grunted thank you. I said you are welcome. There were no clothes available in the assessment unit, just a few bits and bobs people might have left in, I found some clothes and a man's pair of shoes and socks and left them at the end of the bed. She got up early got dressed, and off she went, I felt at least she will be comfortable for a while.

I was on day duty there for a few weeks, the staff was mixed, the ward sister used to go to lunch each day with one of the male nurses. We would say to him, "Take your time so we could enjoy a cuppa when you are gone." My friend was pregnant at the time and was lightheaded in the mornings, the sister went mad when she caught her in the kitchen one morning before tea break, I explained to the sister that she was pregnant, she said, "Why didn't she say so?"

I said, "She was afraid to mention it, you can be very strict." The sister was very nice after that and every morning when Mary arrived she sent her straight into the kitchen for tea and toast, I said to Mary her bark is worse than her bite.

Another nurse, a friend of mine, went far and beyond the call of duty when we were working in 3A, the male admission unit, when the wife and two children of an older patient used to call in after tea twice a week, with her son and a baby girl about a year old. This nurse would ask permission of the wife if she could bathe the baby as she had bought her new clothes. The mother was delighted, the little baby went home sparkling and with clean clothes. My friend did this for months, then her husband died, and we never saw her again but my friend gave her the contact numbers of all the agencies where she could get help. I said to my friend you are so good, she said, "If I can help that mother and child it's a privilege." That's what it was like in the hospital, so many nurses went above and beyond the call of duty, on their day on and their day off for their patients and relatives, so often attending funerals when they had no relatives.

The Union

Our unions worked tirelessly for nurses' and patients' rights. It took many, many years, and with the help of the union, staff managed to get all of your entitlements paid for the duration of sick leave from injury. This agreement was badly needed as we got injured through no fault of our own and ended up being penalized financially. I was on the committee of SIPTU, which was established in 1990 with the merger of the country's two largest unions, the Irish Transport and General Workers' Union and the Federated Workers' Union of Ireland. Both were founded by 'Big' Jim Larkin in the early years of the twentieth century. My dad was also a member of The Irish Transport and General Workers Union now SIPTU, so I guess it was in the blood. I saw how hard he worked for his members and I wanted to do the same. Several submissions were made by SIPTU, the Psychiatric Nurses Association and the Workers Union of Ireland regarding staff shortages which were ongoing, better conditions for patients, special nurses for patients who were suicidal or a danger to themselves and others, pay and conditions for nurses and care staff, compensation for injured staff who were assaulted by patients.

When I started nursing in 1972, there were eighty students each year. This continued for the next few years until the late seventies, so staff numbers were there, though any sick leave, maternity leave, long-term illness, etc., was covered by the existing staff. No extra nurses were ever employed to cover these circumstances. Even when the thirty-nine-hour week was introduced, there were to be at least ten extra nurses to facilitate this, but it never happened. The current staffing levels had to cover this reduction in working hours as well. From the late seventies, the embargo on recruitment came in and student numbers reduced dramatically every year, with eventually only twenty students being recruited annually. The marriage bar was lifted in Ireland in 1973, but for some jobs like ours, it happened in 1977. I got married in 1976 and had to sign away the right for promotion. This affected a lot of nurses who had the experience and years of service, from taking promotion to charge nurse and deputy charge nurse and who had to buy back service at compound interests rates.

This was later resolved in 1988 when the promotion was based on interviews and not on years of service. This barrier to promotion only affected women, which was very discriminatory at that time. Staff shortages were ongoing in the 70s, 80s, 90s, and 2000s. Overtime was introduced in the late seventies to keep the staffing levels up, but in 1982, a directive was issued by the programme manager that all overtime was to cease due to budget restraints. The government were not willing to continue with paying nurses overtime or recruit many new nurses as they would all fall into the pension pot in the future, and the government obviously had their plan in place to close the hospital.

So it didn't surprise me years later when I remembered asking the Matron for holidays to get married in 1976 when she said to me, "Sure, this place could be closed next year." It took nearly forty years later. It made me wonder in later years, when we witnessed the downsizing of the hospital, the reduction in student intake since the mid-seventies, the closure of wards, and community services being slowly developed, that the plan was in place all those years before, but it took so long to implement.

I remembered, as a young girl, all the representations my father made on behalf of members. People would call to the house on his day off to discuss their cases. There were many other issues they had to address: nurses' and auxiliary staff's pay, dinner and tea breaks, holidays, sick leave, marriage gratuity, sleeping in, three hours overtime that was once paid to staff in Grangegorman and Portrane where the ninety-hour fortnight happened in 1962 for six weeks. Many other grievances, members had, were dealt with. Some hospitals had students working for two years without getting to any lectures prior to their exams. Payment for dual-qualified nurses was granted £25 a year in Dublin and £20 in the country. The union in my father's time represented everyone in the hospital, boiler men, carpenters, groundsmen, etc. He gave me his common grievance representations when he retired, not confidential or individual matters. Some old documents are from the 60s before our particular battles from the 70s onwards. I find it hard to believe that now, in 2023, some of the rights our unions worked so hard for have been lost, the retiring age was increased to 65, and acting-up arrangements are much more difficult to attain.

Telephones: DUBLIN [illegible] 63581 Telegrams: "OBU, DUBLIN"

Irish Transport & General Workers' Union

ALL CORRESPONDENCE TO BE ADDRESSED TO THE GENERAL SECRETARY

Head Office: 94 MERRION SQUARE,
DUBLIN, 2

IN REPLY QUOTE
M/33

6th February, 1963.

Mr. R. McGuinness,
ARDEE M.H.

<u>General Trained & Dual Trained Nurses (Male)</u>

A Chara,

We acknowledge receipt of yours of 1st instant with reference to above, contents of which we note.

We are to state that there is no regulation which prevents the Local Authority from paying the extra money or prevents the County Manager from recommending such.

From replies received, we are in a position to advise you that in Clonmel, Killarney, Grangegorman and Portrane £25 p.a. is paid and in Enniscorthy and Waterford £20 p.a. extra is paid.

There are no dual trained nurses in Castlerea, Carlow, Cork, Ennis, Letterkenny, Limerick or Sligo.

Sinne, le meas,
IRISH TRANSPORT & GENERAL WORKERS' UNION,
per

General President

Telephones: DUBLIN 63581   Telegrams: "OBU, DUBLIN"

Irish Transport & General Workers' Union

ALL CORRESPONDENCE TO BE ADDRESSED TO THE GENERAL SECRETARY

Head Office: 94 MERRION SQUARE,
DUBLIN, 2

IN REPLY QUOTE M/33

19th February, 1963.

Mr. R. McGuinness,
ARDEE M.H.

Mental Hospital - 3 Hours Overtime.

A Chara,

We refer to your letter regarding above newspaper report and are to advise that the date given and, in fact all the details, are incorrect.

We have no knowledge of where the report originated but we have now been advised that the 90 hour fortnight was made operative in Grangegorman and Portrane on 15th April, 1962.

In subsequent discussions with the Local Authority it was agreed that the operative datewould be 1st March, 1962. The overtime rate was, therefore, paid for a period of six weeks.

Sinne, le meas,
IRISH TRANSPORT & GENERAL WORKERS' UNION,
per

John Conroy
General President.

Telephone: DUBLIN 67233|4

Telegrams: "OBU, DUBLIN"

Irish Transport & General Workers' Union

ALL CORRESPONDENCE TO BE ADDRESSED TO THE GENERAL SECRETARY

Head Office: 94 MERRION SQUARE,
DUBLIN, 2.

IN REPLY QUOTE
M/33

16th March, 1962.

TO THE SECRETARY OF EACH
MENTAL HOSPITAL BRANCH:

A Chara,

We have been advised that the Labour Court will investigate our dispute with the various Mental Hospital Authorities regarding increased wages, reduced working hours and increased annual leave on Monday, 2nd April, at 3 p.m.

In view of the short time before the hearing, we would request that you let us have all particulars requested in our letters of the 26th ult., and 9th inst.

Examples of recent increases to other Local Authority employees which are greater than 12% would be very helpful. When giving same, please let us have the present and previous salary in each case.

Sinne, le meas,
IRISH TRANSPORT & GENERAL WORKERS' UNION,
per

Edward Browne

Vice President.

EB

Telephone: DUBLIN [illegible] Telegrams: "OBU, DUBLIN"

Irish Transport & General Workers' Union

ALL CORRESPONDENCE TO BE ADDRESSED TO THE GENERAL SECRETARY

Head Office: 94 MERRION SQUARE.
DUBLIN, 2.

IN REPLY QUOTE M/33

18th April, 1962.

TO THE SECRETARY OF EACH
MENTAL HOSPITAL BRANCH:

Salaries - Psychiatric Nurses.

A Chara,

We are to advise you that we have written as follows to the Secretary, Mental Hospitals Joint Industrial Council:

> "On behalf of the Irish Transport & General Workers' Union, the Workers' Union of Ireland and the Irish Women Workers' Union, I am to request that the following motion, in addition to the matter submitted in our letter of 6th ult., be put on the Agenda for the forthcoming meeting of the Joint Industrial Council:
>
> - That the salary scale for female Psychiatric Nurses would be £465 p.a., rising by annual increments of £15 p.a. to £600 and that the differentials as between male and female Psychiatric Nurses would be maintained. -
>
> A meeting of the Joint Industrial Council has been tentatively arranged for 3 p.m., on Wednesday, 9th May."

Sinne, le meas,
IRISH TRANSPORT & GENERAL WORKERS' UNION,
per

General President.

KW

Mr. R. McGuinness,
ARDEE M.H.

Edward Browne

Please see below.

M/33

19th March, 1962.

The Secretary,
Department of Health,
Custom House,
DUBLIN.

St. Brigid's Hospital, Ardee.

Dear Sir,

We are advised that a number of young girls are employed at the above hospital for almost two years and that despite the fact that they are anxious to attend lectures and prepare for their examinations they cannot do so because of Departmental regulations.

We understand that the Local Authority also favours the idea of the girls concerned preparing for and getting their exams and we request that you would favourable consider allowing them to do so.

Your early reply will be appreciated.

Yours faithfully,
Irish Transport & General Workers' Union,
per

Vice-President.

RH

Telephone: DUBLIN 67233/4 Telegrams: "OBU, DUBLIN"

Irish Transport & General Workers' Union

ALL CORRESPONDENCE TO BE ADDRESSED TO THE GENERAL SECRETARY

Head Office: 94 MERRION SQUARE.
DUBLIN. 2.

IN REPLY QUOTE
N/33.

19th November, 1962.

TO THE SECRETARY OF EACH
MENTAL HOSPITAL BRANCH.

A Chara,

We are to enquire as to the position regarding the recruitment of temporary personnel to replace Nursing Staffs absent on Annual Leave, Sick Leave etc. and would appreciate your replies to the questions on the attached at your earliest convenience.

Sinne, le meas,
IRISH TRANSPORT & GENERAL WORKERS' UNION,
per

John Conroy
General President.

Replied 20/11/62.

MH

SENIOR NURSING PERSONNEL

PROPOSED SALARY SCALES

	1,000 Patients and over	Under 1,000 Patients
	MALE	
Head Nurse	£1300 x 36 - 1480	£1180 x 34 - 1350
Deputy Head Nurse	£1230 x 26 - 1360	£1120 x 25 - 1245
Head Night Nurse	£1185 x 25 - 1310	£1095 x 25 - 1215
Tutor	£1185 x 25 - 1310	£1095 x 25 - 1215
Deputy Head Night Nurse	£1160 x 25 - 1285	£1080 x 24 - 1200
	FEMALE	
Matron	£1275 x 34 - 1445	£1150 x 33 - 1315
Deputy Matron	£1200 x 23 - 1315	£1100 x 25 - 1225
Head Night Nurse	£1150 x 25 - 1275	£1020 x 26 - 1150
Sister.Tutor	£1150 x 25 - 1275	£1030 x 26 - 1150
Deputy Head Night Nurse	£1120 x 26 - 1250	£ 980 x 24 - 1100
Housekeeper	£ 800 x 25 - 925	£ 700 x 25 - 825

****

M/33

10th August, 1962.

Mr. John F. Murtagh,
Messrs. John F. Murtagh & Co.,
Solicitors,
25, Eden Quay,
DUBLIN.

Mental Hospitals

Dear Sir,

We have been requested by our members in various Mental Hospitals to see legal opinion on the question of members of the staff being obliged to sleep in the institution to staff the hospital in case of emergency.

In the hospitals concerned the number of staff who ordinarily reside in the hospital is not sufficient, in accordance with local regulations, to provide adequate staff in case of fire etc. The result of this is that members of the staff, including married male staff who ordinarily reside in their own homes, being required to "sleep in" for certain periods without any extra remuneration or time off in lieu.

Our members hold that this is extra duty imposed on them and for which they claim they should be compensated.

The only regulation we can find relating to this is in "The Mental Hospitals (Officers & Servants) Order, 1946, page 55, paragraph (11)(eleven) setting out the duties of the Head Male Nurse; a similar paragraph (13) on page 45 relates to the Head Female Nurse.

Staff Shortages

St. Brendan's Hospital,
P.O. Box 418,
Rathdown Road,
Dublin 7
Tel. : 385844

Your Ref. *Our Ref.*

Prof Ivor Browne,
R.M.S.
St Brendan's Hospital.

18th November 1987

Dear Prof. Browne,

I am writing to you at a time of great stress for the Nursing Staff in the Hospital and the Community. My reason for sending this letter to you is to advise you as R.M.S.: of the serious situation in regard to staffing in the service.

I am to-day short of 100 Nursing Staff for day duty. This is made up of 65 staff left service in the past year and 35 extra staff on night duty. I cannot continue to provide the same level of service with these losses. I am now formally advising you of the situation and I must also advise you that I cannot provide specials or escorts for patients going to General Hospitals on a regular basis.

To make matters even worse this evening I have gross overcrowding in the following wards.

Ward	Beds	Patients.
3A	31	50
3B	23	45
10A	30	39
10B	31	31
[illegible]A	11	21
8B	19	22
	Total Beds 135	Total Patients 208

The above situation is contrary to all good practice of Medicine & Nursing and it should not be allowed to continue.
The Community service is not yet affected but I will be forced to reduce the staff there within the week.

I would appreciate if you could give this matter your immediate attention and I hope you can give me some help and advice.

Yours sincerely,

Chief Nursing Officer.

EASTERN HEALTH BOARD

TELEPHONE 302844 ~~PH~~ ceased

St. Brendan's Hospital,
P.O. Box No. 418,
Rathdown Road,
Dublin 7

YOUR REF:

OUR REF: TK/ML

14th June, 1982.

Chief Psychiatrist.
Each Clinical Director.
Each Chief Nursing Officer.
Mr. McCullough.
Each Senior Executive Officer.

Budget 1982

Dear Mr. Bennett,

The budgetary position has been reviewed in the light of expenditure figures to the end of May 1982 and I regret to say that the position is not satisfactory. The current over run in this programme in annual terms is of the order of £1 million and obviously this trend must be corrected.

By and large there has been a great deal of co-operation from staff in dealing with a very difficult financial position and this has been particular evident on the nursing side. However there is still substantial overtime in the non-nursing areas and in the Central Mental, Dundrum. I am now to request that all non-rostered overtime be eliminated.

It is essential during this holiday season that no substitutes be employed unless absolutely necessary.

Some savings can be achieved on the non pay side. Please arrange to review expenditure and ensure that what is being spent is absolutely necessary in th interest of patients.

I am sure you are aware that the Minister in a recent Dail statement made it absolutely clear that there are no further funds available and that it is a matter for Health Boards and their staffs to live within the allocated budget I am quite satisfied that with the help of all staff we can solve our financial difficulties but it would be regrettable in the extreme of non co-operation by any section of staff was to put jobs of any member of staff at risk. Obviously decisions will have to be made where the half yearly figures to 30th June are available (a copy of these will be sent to you) and I would ask all staff to make a determined effort to correct the unfavourable trend before then. I fully appreciate that what is being asked

/...

will create difficulties but these must be viewed in the light of the possible alternatives which would involve job reduction of a substantial scale.

The contents of this letter should be brought to the attention of staff representatives.

Yours sincerely,

[redacted]
Programme Manager.

The staff shortages continued despite continually moving patients to different wards throughout the hospital if wards were overcrowded. This was very distressing for the patients who may be informed in the morning that they would be sleeping in another unit tonight. It was also very time-consuming for nurses, ringing wards to find out if they had a vacancy to add to their workload. Management's answer for one admission unit was to put a portacabin at the end of a unit to house twelve of their patients every night with one nurse in charge. These practises continued until 1987 when the biggest relocation of patients happened when the lower house was closed with 350 patients, and a three-storey building near the Broadstone units L, M, and N had 140 patients, forty in each ward, nearly 500 hundred patients.

The announcement of the closure of the lower house was a shock to everyone. We were told it was a ministerial order and that the building was no longer fit for purpose. The building we now know is still standing and has been refurbished to the highest standards, but it was not in the government plan to keep it in the psychiatric service. If at any stage during the years, there was any money spent on the upgrading and upkeep of the hospital, it would be a state-of-the-art geriatric hospital. Our older people would not be living in general hospitals or waiting on trolleys for placement in nursing homes. The next buildings to go were L, M, and N, a three-story building located by the Bradstone bus station. There was a very low morale among the staff who were left in the hospital, and who were only informed at the last minute of this further closure. Some staff opted to go with the patients to Cherry Orchard, and St Loman's, the hostels and Area 6, which was a great relief to the patients and their relatives, who knew they would be nurses by the staff who knew them well.

St. Brendan's was particularly affected with large numbers of patient being re-located and once vibrant areas of the campus now lying idle. While many patients were moved to superior accommodation, in some cases the facts belied the publicity.

RTE cameras filmed the closure of Units 1, M and N while Board officials waxed triumphantly of a better quality of life. Nurses who had hastily and hesitatingly moved patients from the area looked sceptically from the windows of the corridor ward, a short walk from the bulldozers, that was the patients new accommodation.

EHB members were treated to a reception in Unit 5C by way of celebrating its closure - oblivious to the fact that the last of those patients had been carried to a disused dance-hall, still on the grounds not 50 feet from the celebrations which was their new home.

Nurses in charge of units had come on duty on another occasion to find the doors to the unit locked and bolted. It has been closed, with on consultation, overnight.

Staff were assembled at short notice (two hours) to be addressed by the Programme Manager, SHCP, the Medical Director and the C.N.O. They were informed that a unit would be transferred off campus to offer the building as emergency accommodation to ease the outcry following the death of two homeless persons.

This was the time when management and the health board were in the process of reducing jobs and the beginning of the closures of the hospital, slowly but surely. One of the admission units, 10-A, was closed in 1992, due to a flea infestation largely caused by lack of maintenance. No staff or patients could be left there during fumigation. Staff were given a firm commitment that it be refurbished and retained as a unit within the hospital. It was reopened after a short time as beds were badly needed. In 1992, integration was introduced in the hospital with male and female nurses working together in some wards. In May 1992, staff were moving out to the community where high and low support hostels were opened in Area 6, which incorporated parts of Finglas, North Circular Road, Aughrim Street, and Blanchardstown. I suppose we didn't know at that time it was all part of the bigger picture of closing St Brendan's. In some ways, it was nice for patients to live in a more homely environment, but some of these hostels were mini units of the hospital that had to be staffed by nurses and care staff day and night.

In 1993, there was a submission to the then minister, Mr Brendan Howlin, TD. regarding violence against nurses, staffing levels, escorts (bringing patients for outpatient appointments in general hospitals or transfers to other psychiatric facilities), and compensation arrangements for nurses who were assaulted, sometimes ending their careers in nursing. The only way for nurses to get compensation was to go to the courts, which were long and costly, and they were out of pocket for years waiting for the outcome, with medical expenses they had to pay, often having to get loans from the credit union. I had to get a loan of 750 euros for a CT neck and soldier scan when I was injured, as private health insurance companies did not cover it at the time. Sometimes cases were settled at the last minute on the steps of the high court.

Top psychiatric hospital faces total shutdown

By Donogh Diamond

ONE OF the country's largest psychiatric hospitals faces a total shutdown in a fortnight, after nurses voted to restart industrial action to force increases in staffing after a series of assaults on the wards.

At a packed meeting last night, nurses at St Brendan's psychiatric hospital in Grangegorman, Dublin, rejected the results of negotiations held in the wake of a strike six weeks ago as inadequate, and voted to recommence action in 14 days unless there was a "radical improvement" in the settlement terms.

The industrial action involved will be an "indefinite strike", the general secretary of the Psychiatric Nurses' Association, Des Kavanagh, confirmed today.

The dispute centres on the care of "special" patients in crisis, who require one-to-one nursing, and a demand for a 39-hour week.

The union says that staff have been taken off other wards to cater for the demands of specials, leaving the wards understaffed and nurses more exposed to assaults.

The present rostering system means that staff actually work a 40-hour week, then are given four hours off every month, instead of working a 39-hour week. But staff are not available to cover the absent nurses when they take these breaks, says the union.

Twelve new nursing posts were created by the Eastern Health Board after the 48-hour strike in April, said Mr Kavanagh, but the assaults have continued and the staffing situation would continue to deteriorate as the peak holiday period appraoched.

Psychiaric nurses see verbal abuse, or a push or a shove, as "part of the territory", he said, but there had been seven assaults in the six weeks since the strike where staff had to be sent for X-rays.

Of those, five suffered actual physical damage, with broken teeth, cut lips or heavy bruising, and two returned to work without treatment.

On one recent Saturday, the hospital had been 14 nurses short, he said.

He appealed to the board to give enough funding to the hospital to ensure proper care of patients and safety for its staff.

Mr Kavanagh is going to ask the Labour Relations Commission to intervene as a matter of urgency.

A spokesperson for the Eastern Health Board said that in addition to the extra staff, the chief nursing officer had been given the authority to augment staff on a given day when there was heavy demand from specials, under the interim solution negotiated with the union.

Direct talks had been taking place and there was a provision for referring the matter back to the LRC if the parties failed to reach agreement, he said.

EVENING PRESS
WEDS JUNE 1ST 94

VIOLENCE AGAINST NURSES

TIME FOR ACTION

Submission to the Minister for Health,
Mr. Brendan Howlin, TD,
from the National Council
of SIPTU-Nursing

Tuesday, July 13, 1993.

SIPTU *Nursing*

MINISTER,

This submission is concerned with the problem of violence against nurses.

In October 1992, the Health and Safety Authority published a report on the Health Services. This showed that 11% of all injuries to Health Service workers were a result of assaults. Of these, 71% were accounted for by injuries to nurses as a result of assault. (71% in Health Boards, 76% in other hospitals).

Despite the publicity given to these figures at the SIPTU Nursing Convention in November 1992, and at several other events, these brutal facts have been ignored by the Management of the Service. Indeed, there is a general indifference to Health and Safety issues in the Service. In one Health Board, this Union confronted Management with details of over 85 incidents of violence on staff, other patients or property in a nine month period in one disturbed Ward. A request for additional staff was refused and the issue was generally treated with indifference. There are similar stories in other Hospitals.

Then, in July 1993, three nurses were victims of a violent stabbing.

This gives rise to three issues.

SIPTU SERVICES INDUSTRIAL PROFESSIONAL TECHNICAL UNION

HEAD OFFICE: LIBERTY HALL, DUBLIN 1 TELEPHONE: (01) 8749731

NATIONAL NURSING COUNCIL

LIBERTY HALL, DUBLIN 1. TEL (01)8749731 FAX (01) 8749268

PATRICK J. BRADY National Nursing Official

ST BRENDAN'S BRANCH BULLETIN

3) STAFF SHORTAGES:

The Committee have decided on the following strategy to highlight the staffing problems and a ballot will be held for your approval and involvement in 1994.

a) Information pickets on the Department of Health. The Dail and Eastern Health Board Meetings highlighting the difficulties being caused to staff and patients.

b) Meetings to be organised with the EHB Committee responsible for the Psychiatric Service.

c) Lobbying of Public Representatives particularly those in the Constituency of Dublin Central.

d) Groups with an interest in patients welfare such as Mental Health Associations, Schizophrenia Associations, Aware, Simon Community etc. to be made aware of the difficulties.

e) Patients relatives to be briefed on the conditions in which patients have to live.

In 1994 we had the nurses' strike took place, having exhausted all avenues to secure pay agreements for nurses and better conditions for patients. The strike lasted for three and a half weeks, and being on the strike committee, we worked so hard during that time, maintaining skeleton staff on each unit, having people on standby for emergencies day and night shifts, manning the picket line and ensuring everyone was safe. Our allocation staff continued in that role as they were the experts at rostering, and to be fair, everyone was very cooperative with the strike. I spent nearly three weeks in the hospital every day and two nights. I hardly got home for a day, I had to get my children looked after, as did many of my colleagues. Most of us could not pay our mortgage that month and had to go to our mortgage lender to take a month or two off our payment agreement to keep a roof over our heads and our children cared for. We believed that it was our only recourse to obtain better pay for nurses and better living conditions for patients.

After all the negotiations, I felt we were let down by our unions. They gave in to government demands with little benefits for staff and patients. When that strike was over, there were clauses in the agreement that were not realized for years later, like the retirement age raised to sixty-five years instead of fifty-five years, which came into effect eventually and affected a lot of the younger nurses, not the people on the negotiating team who were all near enough to retiring age, there was also a clause never to strike again. Our unions assured us, at that time, that this was the best conditions we could achieve. One day, my husband was on the picket line, and the secure unit was in mayhem. The patients were all supportive of the nurses. One particular patient was causing an uproar, he said, "Get nurse Walshe in here, and I'll do whatever he says." He was called in off the picket line and explained to the patient that he needed to do what the nurses on the ward asked him to do, and he hoped to be on duty soon again. The patient agreed and they all settled down. Nurses spent as much time with patients as they spent with their families, apart from their annual holidays, which again had to be fought for over the years. In my father's time in psychiatric nursing, annual leave was two weeks a year. When I started nursing in 1972, it was five weeks a year.

Our unions fought for the Castlerea formula, which was payment for travel allowances and community allowances for nurses working in the community. The introduction of the thirty-nine-hour week, pay parity for pensioners who had left the service and a compensation package for nurses and auxiliary staff who were injured in the course of their duty. The Health and Safety representative updated issues of concern in the hospital and other areas, which could be very difficult as management was not always supportive. Being on union committees or Health and Safety representative was a thankless job. There was no payment, just the satisfaction of knowing that someone had to stand up for the rights of staff and patients.

In 1984, the rehabilitation/resocialization service was opened under the care of Dr Michael Corry. The funding for this project was subsidized by the European Social Fund 55% and 45% by the Eastern Health Board, which allowed for the training of nursing staff in particular skills in rehabilitation. This project was ongoing for several years with the ambition of discharging twenty patients every six months, staff volunteered to be part of this project. This project took quite a few nurses out of the current staffing. It went very well for a few years, eventually the patients who were deemed suitable for rehabilitation were relocated into community areas under agreement which provided for variable starting and finishing, outside of normal starting and finishing times (6am and 5pm). Strike action commenced after the unions claimed management had refused to abide by agreed grievance procedures after unilaterally withdrawing the flexitime arrangements.

FH

St Brendan's - *Unions Want Staffing Hike After Strike*

The first management-union meeting to follow the recent strike over staff levels at Saint Brendan's psychiatric hospital is set to take place this Friday where demands for further staffing will top the agenda for the PNA and SIPTU.

The vast majority of the 260 members of the PNA were on strike for a total of 52 hours at the end of week before an interim settlement was agreed providing for the immediate appointment of ten extra nurses.

The chief nursing officer will also have the discretion to recruit additional staff for short-term needs, including situations where consultants advise that patients require one-to-one nursing. It was also agreed that around 23 PNA nurses who continued to work during the strike would be paid for their work.

Under the Nurses Act, the psychiatric nurses could not leave the wards unless relieved by management. Not surprisingly, given the scale of the walk-out by the PNA nurses, it was decided that a certain number had to be kept on. Some nurses ended up working between 36 and 40 hours continuously as a result.

It was also agreed that none of the staff would be reported to the Fitness to Practice committee or any disciplinary body. But the main provision in the agreement which ended the PNA strike was the willingness to engage in further talks on staffing.

Legal Challenge?

The 118 SIPTU members continued to work throughout the strike but did vote to hold a strike ballot this week. It appears that the strike notice not only took management by surprise, prompting questions over the effective communication of strike notice to all concerned parties, as required under the 1990 Industrial Relations Act. Any move by SIPTU members to support the strike called by the PNA could have left SIPTU open to legal challenge.

As the possibility of SIPTU participation increased with the decision to hold a ballot, there were genuine fears about how the hospital could be supervised and the army was placed on standby. But the relatively small size of the army personnel available in such a situation would have provided possibly insurmountable difficulty. Had a full scale all-out strike transpired, the ability of the army to take over the duties of 330 nurses would have been seriously open to question and there was clearly relief among most of the nurses, hospital managers and families of the patients that this did not come to pass.

And in strictly industrial relations terms, it would have once again increased the pressure for the introduction of a code of practice for essential services, as psychiatric nursing must be considered. As of now, not one employment in what could be deemed essential services has such a code in place.

Twenty Posts?

The ten point agenda for the direct talks between the Eastern Health Board and the two unions will concentrate on full replacement of nurses taking leave as a result of the 39 hour week and the replacement of eleven nurses on long term sick leave. The unions estimate that it would take a further eight nurses to ensure full replacement of staff under the 39 hour week so this would appear to place their demand at around twenty further posts.

The direct talks have been given a timetable for progress and it was agreed that outstanding matters are to be referred to the Labour Relations Commission no later than May 9. But it is understood that the conciliation officer at the Labour Relations Commission who engineered the return to work settlement, Mr Aidan Bunyan, made it clear that serious negotiations in a positive spirit were expected from the direct talks beginning this Friday.

FH

DIT - *Union Submits Proposals to Avert Strike*

The Department of Education was earlier this week considering settlement terms proposed by IMPACT, which has threatened to withdraw all its 200 members in the DIT colleges from next Tuesday in a row over qualifications for new jobs.

Three new principal officer posts have been sanctioned by the

the responsibility of Dr Corry. So, hostel accommodation was acquired for these patients with input from nurses and other disciplines. Eventually, in the nineties, the project was exhausted, and the unit was then called the Rehabilitation Unit, Unit-23, with an open door policy. The patients who resided there were a mixture of long stay patients and patients for rehabilitation with the possibility of moving out to community hostels. Some of these hostels were run by nurses and some were semi-independent with nursing input. It was dreadful that in one of these hostels, two ladies were murdered. I knew these ladies, they were gentle and kind and would not harm anyone.

Speaking on *Today* with Sean O'Rourke on RTÉ, Mr Bailey said that the day he went to the scene would remain forever with him.

Units 3A and 3B

"It was the most horrific crime scene I've ever visited and something that will stay with me for the rest of my life. The ferocity and anger visited on those two elderly ladies, innocent ladies, was frightening to look at."

I was then sent to a very busy admission unit 3B, the new unit as it was called then, even though it was built in the early sixties, with forty-one beds upstairs female unit, and thirty beds downstairs the male admission Unit 3A staffed by male nurses at that time. The admission units had a mixture of acute admissions and some long-stay patients who could not be discharged or placed in other settings. I really liked this unit, it was so busy the day flew by, the charge nurse was really nice, and there was a mixture of staff nurses, attendants, and domestic staff. There were eight consultants and eight junior doctors who treated these patients. It was divided into catchment areas Dublin 2, 4, 6, 8, and 1, 3, 9, and 11. Whatever catchment area you were admitted from determined which consultant would be treating you, and they all had their team meetings on different days. There were young and old people admitted to this unit with all kinds of diagnoses: acute depression, schizophrenia, anorexia, sexual abuse, trauma anxiety, nymphomaniacs, psychopaths, obsessional compulsive neurosis, sociopaths, endogenous depression, and other mixed diagnoses.

The charge nurse in this unit was a great cook and when somebody was leaving, she always found time to cook a lovely meal for them. We covered her duties when she cooked and always had two sittings to ensure the patients were looked after. I came back from holidays to this unit, one morning in the observation ward, which had ten beds, and it was covered in litter around one patient's bed. I went to tidy up and the charge said to me, "Don't touch that area." I was surprised. She told me that the lady had OCD (obsessive convulsive neurosis) about cleanliness, and they were using desensitizing techniques to help her. She was making progress, as she was tolerating some dirt and untidiness around her. She had been making her children eat their dinner over the bin at home in case they would mess up the table or floor. It took a lot of time and work with her, but she was discharged home with techniques to help her overcome this problem.

Another evening, I was just coming back from my tea break when I heard shouting as I was going up the stairs to the unit, and a body passed me on the way down. One of the ladies had jumped off the bannisters. I went to investigate. She had broken a tooth and seemed to have injured her arm and foot. She was conscious and giving out madly. I thought, *oh my god, now she will have to go to Jervis Street Hospital and sure enough, I had to go with her.* I didn't mind, only I was feeling so sick. I was twelve weeks pregnant and still getting sick, but that didn't matter. I had to go, off we went and while we were waiting to be seen in casualty, the stench of alcohol was terrible.

They had two cubicles for people who were very intoxicated with mats on the floor. I felt sorry for the poor nurses who had to check on them regularly, especially as they were either out for the count or agitated. At least they had security guards on hand, which we never had. We were in a line of cubicles divided by curtains, the patient was on a trolley, there wasn't even a chair for me, I was hanging over the sink, splashing my face, I felt faint. Luckily, I had a good relationship with this patient and she shouted for someone to get me a chair. We were seen pretty quickly then, I think they were more concerned they would have to replace me. She needed stitches to her lip and a plaster of Paris on her arm and her foot, these showed fractures on x-rays.

I phoned our ambulance and we got back to our unit quickly. She was very apologetic, I said just talk to us if you feel like doing that again, and she promised she would. There was another lady in the unit whose children were in care and was very worried about them. She was only twenty and had two children, there was no boyfriend around. The kids were placed in care as she could not look after them herself. She had a lot of social problems and anxiety. She would visit them when the social worker could arrange it. When she returned after every visit, she would be very upset and would usually do something like hitting someone or cutting herself, anything to be sedated to block out the memory.

Her situation was terrible for her own sake, she had no family support, nowhere to live, and she was hard to engage in any form of therapy. Her children remained in care and she continued to self-harm. She refused counselling, so she ended up in and out of the hospital for years. It was very difficult to see people like her, who maybe with a lot of support may have been able to change her life but she refused all help. I had two children at the time and couldn't imagine not being able to have them with me every day and see them grow up. We tried our best to help her, but sometimes you realize you cannot help someone who would not make any effort to change.

We had some ladies who used to bring drugs into the unit on their return from a day pass. One lady we knew always tried it. The charge nurse asked us to find the drugs, we searched her, her bed, her locker, and no sign of the drugs. I said, "We should trace her steps from the minute she came back to the ward." I remember she had asked to use the toilet before going to her dormitory, so I decided to check there again. Nothing was visible except when I lifted the lid of the cistern, there was a plastic bag with the drugs, a good result at least, no other patient would get them. This lady was in the hospital for a few years, she was eventually discharged.

I worked in this unit for a few years as there was always a vacancy when I was due back from holidays or maternity leave. I had my third baby, Laura, in 1983, the 13th of February. She was born at 11.55 p.m., just before Valentine's Day. She was beautiful, another little redhead, life went on, and we got very busy with our three children. My two other children adored her as there was a three-year gap. They were a great help minding her. I always kept each new baby in our bedroom until they were a year old, then I would move them into their own room to sleep without the interruption of us going to bed and getting up so early. She was in our room until she was thirteen months old. We felt it was safe enough to move her into her own little bedroom, where we would not disturb her going to bed. The last thing we did every night was to check each child, and always left their bedroom doors ajar so we would hear them if they stirred in the night.

One day at work in this unit 3B, which was over the male admission unit 3A, one of the lads was leaving, and as usual there was a doo for him. My friend asked if my husband and I would go, I wasn't really too keen and said, "If we could our usual babysitter, we could go for a short while." So when I phoned my husband, it was all arranged, and he met me there at the hotel. It was on the north side of the city and on our way home. We stayed for two hours, left our friend home, and got home around 11:30. My husband said he would drive the babysitter home and I went upstairs to check on the children. I went into Laura's room, she was in her cot face down. She always slept on her tummy but I couldn't hear her breathing. I lifted her and she wasn't breathing and was rigid. My heart sank, I started screaming. I put her down into her cot and crossed the road to my friend, who quickly came back with me. I cradled her in my arms, she was definitely gone, with a trickle of blood at the side of her mouth. Someone called an ambulance and the guards. My husband was torn with grief like I was. The ambulance man just took her out of my arms and went off in the ambulance. They said we could follow to Temple Street Children's Hospital. My friends stayed with Mark and Fiona who remarkably slept through it all. When we got to Temple Street Children's Hospital, we waited for hours, not knowing what was happening. I just wanted to hold my baby girl.

Eventually, a nun came out to us and said they would bring her in. She handed her to us and told my husband to mind her head. He said, "I know how to hold my own child." But she insisted he mind her head. Little did we know, that night or for fifteen years later, what they had done to her They had done a post-mortem and taken away all of her organs and stuffed her with cotton wool or whatever. I asked the nun if we could dress her for the funeral, she said, "No not at all. You are both too stressed. We normally do that, just bring in whatever outfit you want her dressed in." We had no choice. Never in a million years did I think they could take her organs without our permission.

The next few days were like a maze. We had to tell Mark and Fiona, who were six and nearly four, that their baby sister was gone to heaven with holy god. I don't think they could understand, and neither could I. A child who was loved and wanted had to die for no reason. I thought of all the little children who were in care, or neglected, or physically or sexually abused and were allowed to live. I felt so angry that even Mickey, our family priest, could not console us. She was only fourteen months old. My friends Teresa and Mick called out to the house the next night. They felt they had to come in person. Teresa just hugged me, there was no consolation. We had the funeral three days later when the hospital released her.

All of our friends from the hospital came nurses, doctors, care staff, and maintenance staff, for a little child, it was a big funeral. We buried her in Swords Cemetery. We insisted on a double grave for which we had to get another loan, but we refused to have her buried in the angel's plot in Glasnevin as suggested by the nun. We wanted a grave near us that our children and relatives could visit. I must say we got such support from our parents, relatives, and work colleagues. Counselling was never even mentioned at that time. When Laura died it nearly killed us, especially Billy. He was never the same person after that, he couldn't bear the loss. It left such a hole in our hearts that could never be fixed but we had to go on and look after our other two children.

My husband went back to work on a Sunday and I got a phone call from Mickey to say his dad had died on the 13th of May, just thirteen days after Laura, who died on the 1st of May. I think it broke his heart too, we went down the country to the funeral with the children. I never felt so alone in my life, it was all about Dan, Billy's dad. I thought he was seventy-six, he had lived his life, unlike Laura. It was like 13 days later, and she wasn't mentioned. I just cried, Billy was in the pub afterwards with all the relatives and friends, as was the custom. I just brought my kids for a walk, I had to keep going for them. I'm sure all the relatives and friends hadn't forgotten Laura that day, she was mentioned at the funeral mass for Dan, and that was it. No one asked me how I was, how was I coping, or how did I feel. I was just going through the motions, I cried all night, no one heard, they were all too busy with Dan's death. I had an inconsolable hole in my heart, an emptiness that no one could feel or understand. The sheer emptiness of losing our little daughter, a little person who was walking and talking that we had buried ten days ago and would never see again.

We went home the following day, I was exhausted as I still could not sleep, going over in my mind did we change her food, and had we not noticed something, but she was happy, healthy, and walked at ten months. She could stand up in her cot and call you if she wanted something. It took seven months to get the post-mortem results. There was no cause, the verdict was sudden infant cot death, no other explanation.

I went back to work after another week. I really was still too traumatized to work, but I had to because there was no extended leave at that time. Everyone was so kind, the patients knew, as I had been in that ward 3B for a long time. The patients all gave their condolences, even the maddest of them. One lady told me she lost two babies to TB, maybe she never got over the grief. I just went through the motions for weeks, I said to the charge nurse just give me the mundane tasks, which had to be done but were routine, and you just done automatically.

After weeks of torture and sleepless nights, my husband suggested we have another child. I didn't want to rush it and never had any problem getting pregnant. I remember one of the older nurses saying to me one day, "All my husband has to do is leave his trousers at the end of the bed and she would be pregnant," I laughed and thought there's no mystery in that. Within three months I was pregnant again, I was delighted as

I knew my husband would never get over Laura's death if we did not have another child. It was the usual, I was sick again, losing weight, people at work thought it was the grief, and so I had to tell them. They were all delighted too, and were so thoughtful. The charge nurse said to me one evening, "Come out for coffee and a sandwich for our tea break."

I said, "What's the point I can only drink water, or I could have chips." So she ordered chips and a glass of beer, I thought I'll try and sip it, but I could not believe it stayed down. She said, "Don't you know that beer is an antiemetic?"

So the following day, I went to the supermarket and bought non-alcoholic beer Caliber it was at that time. Every day, I would bring six bottles of this non-alcoholic beer with me to work. The deputy matron, on her morning rounds, used to pop her head into the tea room and I would be drinking beer. When I explained it to her she said, "Drink as much of it as you can, you might put on some weight." Sure enough I did, so I had that for the first four months until I could drink tea again, etc.

The pregnancy went great after that and I had the usual long two-day labour and Liam was born ten pounds eleven ounces, a bruiser, but the most unusual thing was he had black hair. Everyone was so delighted for us after Laura's death the previous year.

My friend, the charge nurse, the great cook, insisted she would do the buffet for his christening. She was brilliant and cooked everything to her usual perfection. We had plenty of meals she would cook for us on special occasions, she even asked me to take the pips out of the grapes for her fruit cocktail dessert, there were no seedless grapes at that time. She was a great nurse and would have been a brilliant chef. I was exhausted after the birth and I don't know what I would have done without her help, I will never forget her kindness. Liam was only a week old but it coincided with Mark's communion, and you could not ask the relatives to come up from the country again a few weeks later. So our family priest Mickey said he would do the christening after the communion, and so he did.

What a day, I was exhausted but Liam was very good and handed around to everyone, we had the buffet in the house and the weather was great, so all the kids were outside in the sunshine. I continued to work in the admission unit until my next holidays and was back there again after that. Life was good again at home even though there was still a hole in my heart that's still there and never goes away. I know Laura's death broke Billy's heart, he thought having another baby would fill that empty place but it never did. You never get over such a tragedy, you just learn to live with it. We were busy minding our two children, and having another baby helped us to move forward, but you never forget your lost little girl, not even for a single day. You just had to continue living and keep going for your other children, who were only four and six at that time.

There was another unusual lady in this unit, she said she was abused as a child and she believed all of her problems were as a result of this, and she was like many people who were admitted because they could not cope with the trauma. But there were so many others that we know suffered in silence for years, or maybe their whole lifetime, without getting help. She was a likable character, but god knows she wore us out with her constant overdoses, cutting herself, swallowing glasses and batteries. She would inflict the most horrific injuries on herself. She would be sent to the Mater Hospital and had many surgeries to remove these items glass, batteries, knives, spoons and drug overdoses. She actually cut her abdomen and took out her intestines one night and put them on the bed, the nurses wrapped her up in sheets and got an ambulance to the Mater. The surgeons in the Mater were getting intolerant of her constant presentations, but this was the last straw. They eventually put a light mesh in her abdomen under her skin to prevent this constant cutting of herself.

When I was a deputy charge nurse in this unit, I made a bargain with her, I asked her if she was going to do anything else, as she probably would, that she would do it elsewhere and phone me from whatever hospital she was in, and I would send all her belongings to her for her hospital stay. We agreed and the next time she got herself admitted to the Mater Hospital, I sent her things down to her. She didn't do anything in the unit again while I was deputy charge. She had done the most awful things in the past, all harmful to herself. Many different therapies had been tried with her but none were very successful. I think she wanted the hospital to be her home and continued with these behaviours. It's hard to think that anyone would want to stay indefinitely in the hospital because they felt safe, and did not want to live in the outside world, she was one of them.

One particular evening I was walking through the dormitories around 7 p.m. checking everyone was ok before the night staff would come on duty. I went into her six bedded dormitory, she called me and said she wasn't feeling well. I said, "You know our bargain?"

She said, "Yes, but this is different." She was a bit breathless and in pain. I said I believe you, it was genuine. I told her I would get the doctor and ring an ambulance. She was admitted to the Mater, she had a clot in her lung. They kept her for two days. When she returned, she thanked me. I said, "You know, I'm not surprised this happened. You have been doing so much damage to yourself for years now something was bound to give." I think she got such a fright she may have seen the light, for a short time anyway.

There were some ladies who attended Holotropic Therapy, which was conducted by Professor Ivor Browne, where people would regress back to stressful trauma in their lives and work through the situation again. Some patients found it helpful, some found it very distressing. Professor Browne also used hypnotherapy, this particular lady whom he hypnotized to wake up in the morning after a good night's sleep when Mary clicked her fingers. Mary was the deputy who worked on my opposite shift. I clicked my fingers the next morning, as instructed and she didn't wake up.

Then it dawned on me that he should have said to her that the nurse in charge would waken you when she clicked her fingers. I went to his office and told him of the dilemma. I said, "We work day on and day off. Mary is not on duty today." So I suggested he rephrase it to the nurse in charge, he laughed and came to the ward and changed the words to suit, he said try it. I did and it worked. He laughed again saying he forgot to factor our shift work in. I said to him, "You know, Professor that we don't all work nine to five." To be fair he didn't either, when he was conducting his halotropic therapy, it would be seven or seven thirty before the patients were escorted back from the Protestant Church where it took place. One of the male nurses from 3A downstairs phoned me one evening after the patients had returned from holotropic therapy, saying, "One of your ladies is screaming her head off at the end of our unit outside."

I said, "Just leave her, she is after attending a session in the protestant church, she will come in when she is ready."

This admission unit was the largest admission Unit with 41 beds, with old and younger patients all mixed up together and was very difficult to manage. We made several efforts to separate the age groups and to have a day ward for each group. Sometimes, when a younger patient might be unwell they would take their anger out on an older granny, so separating them was the best option to keep the peace. It worked fairly well.

Oftentimes, older people were very paranoid on admission and very reluctant to take medication in tablet form. One such lady refused point blank, and we did not want to sedate her with an injection, so we used the clear liquid medication Serenace. I made sure to be there at her table in the mornings before she had her cup of tea. I put her dose in the cup before pouring her tea in. She watched me like a hawk, but luckily, she didn't notice as it was a clear liquid. After a few days, she said to me you don't have to sit with me at mealtimes, "I'm perfectly capable of having my own meals without you."

I said, "Fine." She agreed to take tablets then as her paranoia had lessened, she got well and returned home after a few weeks. I thought there is usually a gentle way to help older people.

There were a few au pairs admitted from other countries who were working in Ireland for the summer. There was one young Spanish girl with no English. She was terrified and very paranoid, she refused to take medication. I remember the charge nurse said, "We will just have to hold her down and sedate her."

I was not happy with this, the poor girl was so frightened in a strange environment, with strange people, and didn't know what was happening to her. I said, "Let me have some time with her." I sat at the end of the bed saying nothing, eventually, she moved closer to me. I held her hand and signalled it's going to be ok. I had to do everything in sign language. I had a little container in my hand with the tablets in it, I raised it to my mouth so she would know what she had to do. I had a glass of water in my other hand, she took the tablets and the water. I got her to lie down slowly, told her everything would be ok in signals and she fell asleep. I kept a good eye on her until she woke up again, reassuring her all the time. She took her medication from me three times that day. I told her I would be off tomorrow as we worked day on and day off and wrote the day on a piece of paper for her when I would be on duty next, she seemed to understand. We arranged for an interpreter to come the next day to talk to her.

Every day I was working, she was delighted to see me and I was delighted she was getting less paranoid. We contacted her father in Spain, he arrived over when she was ready to go home. He was a huge man with a big sombrero hat, had a little English. He thanked us, she gave me a hug and off they went. I just thought to myself, *if that was my daughter in the future, I would like someone to look out for her and spend that little bit of time to reassure her and get her the treatment she needed.*

I remember, as a student years before in that same unit, we had an extremely paranoid and agitated seventy-year-old sprightly lady who was admitted on a temporary form. The charge nurse said to me, "We need your help to sedate her."

I thought, *this would be easy, she didn't look too bad,* until we went to sedate her. I was told to hold that leg, just as I was in place, she managed to take off her stiletto shoe and she rammed it into my head. All I could see was blood everywhere, my blood spurting out of my head. The patient went off to the dormitory after her sedation, it would kick in fairly quickly and we wanted her in her bed. The charge nurse took me into the clinical room. She took out a bottle of dettol and washed off the blood, then she put a few steristrips on the gash. Then she told me, "Now go over to the nurse's home and get cleaned up and come straight back." No anti-tetanus, no are you ok, just be back for lunch. That's just the way it was then, you just had to get on with it. Nowadays you would be sent off to a general hospital to get sutured and a possible scan and an anti-tetanus, and probably sent off work for a day or two.

We got seven weeks holidays at that time and we would usually go to my parents for a few days and go to Billy's parents for a few days if we could get two weeks off together, and do trips to the zoo and local beaches as well. Liam was seven months old now, and we were on holiday in Billy's mother's house in Thurles. I was reading the paper and standing at his mother's aga cooker. I couldn't stand the smell of the paper, I said to Billy, "Smell that."

He said, "There's no smell of that paper."

"Well," I said, "I must be pregnant. It stinks." I never needed any test, I was sick the next day, and here we go again. This was not planned as Liam was just seven months.

Stephen was born when Liam was just fifteen months old, I asked them in the hospital if they could check his breathing as I did with Liam because of Laura's cot death, but Stephen's breathing under a monitor was not as it should be. There were no baby monitors at that time for home use.

I asked if I could buy one, they said no. Cutting a long story short, Stephen was admitted five times to Crumlin Children's Hospital for monitoring and was on medication for four years. 12 midnight, 6 a.m., 12 midday, and 6 p.m., and he had his Neulin levels tested every two weeks to alter the dose as he got older. One of our male nurses was doing his children's nursing there at the time, he said to me, "Don't be rushing over in the morning Lucy, I'll give Stephen his bottle, etc." Not a chance he rang me at home at 9 a.m. to say, "Stephen refused everything, could I come in ASAP."

I said, "I'm on my way." It was such a trek up to James Street and onto the Coombe and then to Crumlin, then parking was a nightmare. I would stay with Stephen all day and my husband the next day, and we got our neighbour to mind Liam. My other friends would mind Mark and Fiona after school.

It was a long four years going over and back to Crumlin with Stephen, but eventually his breathing was fine. In my years of spending time in Crumlin I saw so many parents staying overnight with their children, parents from the country with no place to stay and could not afford hotels. They wanted to be with their children, who were very sick and possibly with limited time to live. So in the end, I wrote several letters to the management of the hospital asking them to facilitate parents from the country to be able to stay in the hospital, eventually they opened a unit for parents to stay with bedrooms, a sitting room, and kitchen, shower, and toilet facilities. Many parents and I brought in baby clothes, and toys for the children's playroom, where some children could spend some time if they were well enough out of the bedrooms as the rooms were very small.

I was still working in this admission unit which was

extremely busy. There were changes for staff and every few years, charge nurses and deputy charge nurses were moved to different wards. The charge nurse I had been working with was moved to a long-stay ward. I was devastated to see her go as she was a great charge nurse and cook. Then a new charge nurse, who agreed to work weekend time, that is, Monday to Friday, 9 to 5. Management thought there would be more continuity if the charge nurses were working 9 to 5. They must have thought nothing happens at weekends, but hospitals are 24/7, and a lot can happen over a weekend, especially if a charge nurse also had a Monday off. The first charge nurse was great, she was sent from Portrane for a year, and things went smoothly. She was adaptable and listened to her staff, who had been working in the unit for years. After her year was up, she got a promotion in her own area in Portrane, so she took her promotion and left.

The marriage bar was lifted in 1997, and the promotion was based on interviews rather than on seniority. I was promoted to Deputy Nursing Officer in 1988 in St Dympna's Alcoholic Unit on the North Circular Road. This was a much better system of promotion as people who were actually interested in running a unit had the opportunity to do so. Prior to this time, it was the seniority system and people had to take charge even if they had no interest or inclination to be in charge. Lots of nurses were happy to stay as staff nurses and do their night duty every six weeks. It was much more profitable moneywise, and it suited some nurses who would get a lot of extra weeks off throughout the year. Every charge nurse needed good staff nurses and most of them were excellent at their work caring for and treating patients, and mentoring students. We also had a lot of school leavers who had completed their leaving certificates and were waiting for college places or apprenticeships who worked in the hospital for a few weeks in the summer. Working in a psychiatric hospital was an eye-opener for them. Some of them were terrified, but once they got used to the wards with all the staff watching out for them, they really enjoyed it, and some decided to do nursing as a consequence.

I spent two years in St Dympna's as a Deputy Nursing officer, with male and female staff. I found this unit very rewarding, helping people with addiction to alcohol, drugs, and gambling and the consequences to those affected and their families. I had spent many terms there in the past, and even though this is the unit I got injured in, just as my term as deputy was ending there. While I worked in the alcoholic unit, I was glad to be able to help so many people. Many people made very successful recoveries, and some did not, but the services were there. It was a specialized service in St Dympna's and aftercare provided in Stanhope Street for the person and their relatives, this service was life-changing for many people. Since its closure, there has not been a similar specialized unit operated by the Health Board, which was a great void in the system of looking after people with addiction to alcohol, drugs, and gambling. There are new services available, but the detoxification process is operated under the general services.

After my two years in St Dy,pna's, I was assigned to 3B as Deputy Nursing Officer in 1990, on the roster of day on and day off, which was customary at that time. Management was making changes to the roster with the introduction of weekend time, nursing officers who would work Monday to Friday, and nine to five. I was asked to take charge of this unit, but it would mean working on weekend time. I had to refuse the promotion as it would disrupt my whole family life, having to get my children minded in the mornings and evenings while my husband was working, and financially it would have cost me money. So a new charge from the hospital, who was a single lady agreed to work that shift, and we still worked as deputies on the day on day off system. So now we had a weekend charge nurse again. I was a deputy on one shift and my opposite number, Mary, on the other shift.

The whole atmosphere of the unit changed, while this lady said she would not be making any changes for a few weeks, until she observed how the unit worked. We said great but it didn't last long, after three days she wanted many changes. She had a very authoritarian attitude, whereas we had a democratic attitude, which the staff appreciated. We took all their ideas on board and came to a general consensus on most matters, and the final decisions were left to the charge nurses after this consultation. I always found that people work better when they are appreciated, their ideas and views listened to, and while I might not always agree with them everyone had their say. We had so many young acute admissions there, from our own catchment area, but also many au pairs who came to Ireland to work for the summer, who needed treatment but needed kindness and empathy from staff. Some of them did not even speak English, and we would have to get an interpreter when they arrived. It could be anyone's young adult with mental health problems.

There were many disagreements with this lady and people found it difficult to work under this autocratic regime. I constantly found myself going between her and the staff, staff, nurses, nurses' aids, and the housekeeping staff. Then, one day, it came to a head, after a year of her management style, a disagreement about the equipment nurses needed to do their job. She was like one of the older charge nurses who felt their stock room was sacrosanct and would not allow staff nurses to get what they needed. We would normally solve our own issues but there was no talking to her, so I phoned the director of nursing, unfortunately he was off that day, so I asked for the assistant director of nursing.

When he arrived, I explained the situation, that she was making it impossible for the nurses to do their work. I asked the assistant director of nursing to sort her out or move one of us to another unit. She couldn't speak, she got such a fright, and she never thought anyone would stand up to her. I could not let this situation go on any longer. It was affecting the welfare of the staff and the patients, and the atmosphere in the unit was completely different when she was off duty. So he told her in no uncertain terms to manage the unit properly and asked me if I wanted the rest of the day off. I said, "No thanks." That would look like she had won to the other staff, whom I supported, so I stood my ground and stayed put.

When the Director of Nursing came to see me my next day on duty, he asked me if I wanted to go to the rehabilitation services. I said, "I would consider it if he had arrangements for her too, that she would have to go first or at the same time, I was not going to be a scapegoat." This happened quite a lot in nursing, promote someone to get the situation solved. Management was not very good at taking people to task who were intimidating staff and patients. They would always look for the easy way out. She took holidays and I went to the rehabilitation services the following week in 1993, Unit 23. She was transferred to another unit, a male unit, with male staff nurses where conflict might be less likely to arise.

The Rehabilitation service had been started by Dr. Michael

Corry in the 80s with EU funding. This project was to allow for training of staff to facilitate patients living in houses in the community with the support of nurses and housekeeping staff. This project was in keeping with what was happening in other Western countries with high crime rates, widespread abuse of alcohol and drugs, unemployment, and disadvantaged youth, which led to an urgent need for a different type of challenge to mental health services. So it was decided to go ahead with this project, I knew several nurses who were very enthusiastic about this and volunteered to be part of this new service. Several houses were purchased for the relocation of patients after a training programme in the rehabilitation unit which I was to be deputy in. I thought the change would be good. The rehabilitation unit was in 1992 incorporated into the hospital service with the staff who had been trained in rehabilitation rotating from the hostels to the unit on a regular basis.

When I was assigned there, this programme had been running for eight years, hostels were in situ, some with housekeepers, and some supervised by nurses. In the previous years, anyone that could have been moved out of the hospital were living in these hostels. However, the move to continue moving people out to hostels continued. This next group of people were in high-support hostels with nursing and care staff on duty, so basically, there were mini wards in the community. The vision for independent living that had been started by Dr. Corry who had now moved on, was taken over by another consultant. The whole emphasis was on multidisciplinary teams with nurses, psychology, occupational therapists, art therapists and a social worker. There would be weekly meetings on each patient's progress, family members could be involved if they wished in the patient's care plan, but a lot of these patients had no relatives, or the relatives were not interested in being involved. Space for running programmes was limited, and as the initial funding had run out it was very difficult to make a success of the programmes.

It was probably a lot easier for the other disciplines to do their sessions, whereas nurses had a lot more to do in the unit, which was sparsely staffed for a mixed unit with twenty-four patients. The consultant felt that more programmes should be done with the patients. I said, "Ok but whoever draws up a programme, needs to supervise it." With no disrespect to any discipline, the occupational therapists would, for e.g., drew up a shaving programme with twenty steps. I looked at it and said, "It looks ok but you will do it with the patient, not me."

They said, "Would 11 o'clock be ok?"

I said, "No the patients are up at 8 and breakfast at 8:30, so 9 o'clock would be fine, you're starting time for your work."

So two of them arrived at nine and went through their twenty steps and finished two patients by 11 a.m. They were to do it for the five days of the week, but two days seemed to be enough for them. The next week at the meeting, they said they could not do it, so I got electric razors for all the patients for those who were not able to shave themselves. The occupational therapists had different roles than nurses and involved different tasks, some cooking, self-care, socialisation, like bringing the patients to constructed sessions and going out for coffee, using the busses, and sometimes going on outings to the zoo or cinema, this was great for the patients as we nurses had all the nursing duties to do and would not have time for these services. The particular group we has in the unit would be difficult to place as they had too many psychiatric issues. Any of these patients that we were able to move out were most likely to go to high-support hostels. We managed as best we could to go with the rehabilitation, but several of the patients there were long stays and had not engaged with any programmes. There were many inappropriate admissions to this unit, patients who had been in Dundrum Mental Hospital for many years and somehow now were deemed suitable for rehabilitation.

My husband happened to be the deputy charge in the block, the secure unit on the male side, with six male nurses as the staff quota per day. One of these patients, who was transferred there from Dundrum, was in the process of being assessed for the rehabilitation unit. He posed no problem in the block as he could see there were six nurses and care staff, the psychiatrist in charge of our unit was intending sending him to our unit. My husband advised me of his severe forensic history and feared for our safety if he was transferred, as I had only one staff nurse and one care staff, and would often be on my own with a care staff at mealtimes in the evenings when the weekend charge nurse was off and the staff nurse might be on hours off.

Before the transfer took place, I had decided that if the consultant transferred him, I would not stay there as it would be too dangerous. She relented and had him assessed again by the psychiatrist in Dundrum, and on reflection, he said that he was totally unsuitable and he was discharged back to Dundrum. There were many times nurses had to make a stand. We would be the ones on duty if things blew up and many a time, they did. We did not have personal alarms or security, and you would be lucky to get to the office phone to ring for help. This happened to me twice in this unit. This was an open unit and people were likely to wander in, most other units were locked.

A patient from a hostel called in for the seven o'clock tea break, which the patients had every evening. This person has been transferred from the psychiatric unit in another Hospital. He had attacked someone and after a stretch in the block, and then time spent in the rehabilitation Unit, he was then transferred to a hostel. I was in the kitchen after the patients had their tea, Paddy came in and stared vividly at me, I said to him, "Go back to the hostel you've had your tea." He swirled around and fell face down on the floor. It was a hard blow as the kitchen was tiled, then he started fitting. I had read in his notes that, that is when he had attacked someone in another psychiatric hospital when having a fit. I had to save him, he was choking. He used to wear a duffle coat buttoned under his chin, I tried to open it, and it was so tight that he was going blue. I pulled his dead weight onto his back, got the hood open and then his shirt open. I was sweating with the effort. As soon as his colour began to return and he had stopped fitting, I rolled him on his side and ran to the end office off the kitchen to ring for help. I had stuck my key in the door in case he revived and came after me. I phoned the office for help as I was alone in the unit, the other nurse was on hours off. I knew none of the patients could hear anything as they were in the sitting room and had the television on high volume. I peeped out the door, checked in the kitchen serving hatch that he was breathing and went up to the office. Help had arrived, and two nurses drafted from other units. They got an ambulance to transfer him to the mater because of his head injury. I was so relieved he was ok, but it took its toll on me, if he had attacked me, I didn't stand a chance.

I had to write the usual incident report again before I went home. The consultant contacted me the next day to say they wanted to do a debriefing meeting. I said ok, but I wanted my friend, the weekend Charge Nurse, to be present. The meeting was scheduled for eleven a.m. We went into the office and the Director of Nursing, the Consultant, the psychologist, the occupational therapists, and a social worker were sitting waiting for us. I was surprised so many people were interested in my welfare.

It wasn't long before the questions, accusations, blame started, "Why were you in the unit on your own?" "Why was a hostel patient in the unit?" etc., etc. I couldn't believe it, it was like a courtroom, and I was on the stand. I listened for a while and thought to myself, *I did nothing wrong, I actually saved a man's life.* So I stood up and said, "That perhaps the management team of the hospital should look at the way they were running the hospital, constantly leaving the nurses short of staff and in danger. Management decided to bring in the thirty-nine hour week, and instead of engaging new nurses to make up the shortfall, the hours off were at the expense of the existing staff. Furthermore," I said, "at least no one died due to my quick thinking. If he did die, you would be facing a much more intensive investigation."

I thanked them for their apparent concern for me and said, "I did not have to listen to any more ridicule," and that maybe they could look at the meaning of a debriefing for future nurses who went over and above their call of duty. So I left and I was delighted my Charge Nurse left with me, she was disgusted with them.

There were some other unfortunate patients in the Unit Two who had been through the industrial schools and farmed out in their teenage years. I followed up on their histories. One occupational therapist had investigated with the Red Cross and we discovered his relatives were in the west of Ireland. We wrote to them to let them know they had a relative in the unit, a brother. They said they did not want anything to do with their brother. We did not tell him as he would be too upset. He got angry with me one day over cigarettes when I was going to my lunch. He had got his quota but wanted more. I was in my car outside the unit, he was roaring at me. I rolled down the window and told him to ask the nurse inside. He kicked my car door so hard he dented it. I drove off to my lunch before the rock he was holding went through the window. I had to go to the ends of the earth before the hospital administrator would agree to pay for the damage to my car.

Another lovely patient who had been in the long-stay units for years was referred to us for rehabilitation. I had read his history that was in the notes. He had been in care since he was two years old, his mother could not look after him and his sister, who was four. He was sent to the Artane industrial school and then to Galway to a farm. He ended up being admitted to Ballinasloe Mental Hospital. He allegedly had set fire to a barn where he had to sleep; he was not given lodgings in the house, and was then transferred back to St Brendan's. I called to see him in a long stay unit 1B and talked to him, I asked him if he would like to come to our ward. He didn't speak much, I spoke to the charge nurse, who knew him well and said he was never any trouble and kept to himself. He agreed to come to us and settled in slowly.

This was an open unit and patients could go out on the grounds if they wanted to. He was not used to this and never ventured out on his own. He has come from the long-stay unit in hospital clothes, he had nothing of his own. At that time, patients were given eight euros a week of comforts money if they wanted to buy treats, but his money was used in a general fund for the ward as he never asked for anything.

I told him this money was his and we would save it for a few weeks and buy him what he wanted. He said he would like his own clothes and a radio, so we saved for a few months, and I asked if he would like to go shopping with me. He said no, you get the clothes, so we discussed what he wanted, I measured him up and got the clothes in my lunch break. I got his anorak, shirts, trousers, jumpers, underwear etc., and the radio. When I got back, he was waiting for me, we went upstairs to his dormitory and he opened the bags. I got name tags too. He started to cry, I thought, *did I get the wrong stuff?* "No," he said, "I have never had my own clothes or anything else."

He was delighted and slowly he started opening up to me, it was quite an effort as he had no confidence in himself, kept his head down. I eventually got him talking and some smiles at last. I often thought life would have been so different for him if he had been adopted and lived with a family. I believe any spirit he had was beaten out of him in his youth, but he was happy with us and came on holidays with us to Wexford to a Vincent de Paul facility, where we, as a group of nurses, brought our unit and hostels, and another unit in the hospital to Wexford for four years in a row, four days each year it was the only holiday they ever had. Other units had gone to a facility in Mornington Co Meath for years prior to that time, they were more independent patients. It was difficult for the nurses to go on patients' holidays, as we had to get our own children looked after for the four days, but the excitement for the patients was wonderful.

The local pub where we used to go at night had a pool table and put on a local DJ for them to dance, and allowed them to have singing competitions between the groups. We went off on the bus every day exploring the sights in the sunny southeast and walked the strand each evening when we got back. Amazingly no one misbehaved or relapsed on the trips. Some of these patients were very talented, but through their illness, they never got back the talent and skills they had before their illness. One such lady was a great sketch artist; her father would visit regularly, and I got to know the family. He would bring in some of her sketches to show me, the expertise and quality were superb. I did painting and art myself but could never compete with her. I tried to encourage her to start her artwork again, I got her equipment, paints, artist pencils, sketch pads, etc., but her skills were gone. She tried but she could not even draw. It was such a pity.

Nurses have great intuition, I was in charge of the unit one particular day when another patient appeared to me to be very volatile. We would normally have gone on two dinner breaks but this day to ensure safety, I suggested we do three lunch breaks. So two nurses would be there at all times. Two nurses went to lunch and all was ok, then I went with the second nurse, and when I got back, the two nurses were sitting outside looking exhausted.

I asked, "What had happened?"

They said, "Take a look at the downstairs dormitory."

I looked in and every bed and wardrobe was upturned and the place was in a terrible mess. The female patient had gone berserk and wrecked the place. They had to get help to sedate her and have her transferred to the block for a week until she settled. I asked them if they were ok, and they said they were

just shocked. There was no talking to her, at least, no one was physically injured again, but the gut feeling you have about someone is usually right, thank god I went with my gut.

This particular lady had been seeing another patient who was a psychopath and sociopath, but she said she loved him. She had been on a contraception injection and started to refuse it monthly. I explained to the consultant, who was not unduly concerned, but I was. This lady could not mind herself, let alone a child. Despite our best efforts to persuade her, she refused contraception and got pregnant. This added another dangerous element to the unit. Her boyfriend came to visit and would invariably start a fight each time with another male patient. In the end, the charge nurse and I, had to get him barred from the unit. She eventually had the child, I had been moved to take charge of a high-support hostel and did not follow the outcome. I do know however that her boyfriend was found dead in the Phoenix Park a year or two later.

This is another unit, the rehabilitation unit that I was attacked in. One patient had gone missing for four days, the Gardaí were informed but he was not found. Then one day, he turned up at lunchtime, just walked in dishevelled and hungry. I offered him dinner which he wolfed down. I was very concerned as he had had no medication when he was missing, and he had schizophrenia and could be very paranoid. I phoned the consultant and asked her to immediately review him, he refused the liquid sedation I offered him, and so I kept my distance. I advised her that we needed more staff or to move him to the block for a few days to resume his medication. She was reluctant to do this, with the result that just as I was going to the dining room where the patients were sitting after their dinner, I put my key in the door to open it, and he made a run for me. God knows who he thought I was. I was about to be thrown through a glass door and wrenched my back to turn my face away, then another patient got between us and saved me from that fate. The patient restrained him with the male nurse, who heard the commotion on his return from his lunch, then nurses arrived to bring him to the block. I did not blame the patient, he had no medication for days and was obviously extremely paranoid and unfortunately, I was the one to get the wrath of his anger. I do blame the consultant for not acting on our well-founded concerns, this attack could have been avoided and I had injured my shoulder and back, and was off sick for a few weeks. I will be eternally grateful to the patient who saved me, as many patients do in nurses' lives in psychiatry.

I subsequently had to have back and shoulder surgery in a year's time despite having physiotherapy and steroid injections etc., which did not work. So once again all of this could have been avoided if nurses were listened to by the consultant. She was a good consultant and felt patients had a right to live their own lives, and that was fine if they were in a fit position to do so, but consultants or even doctors are not usually present when these incidents occur, they order the medication afterwards, after the event, and mostly we would insist on having a PRN dose prescribed that is an emergency dose of medication so that we could avert these situations, people forget nurses are with the patients twenty-four seven and know their moods and can sense a flare up, before any doctor would notice.

I had the extra job of doing all the flower arranging for the church every week and all special occasions, like Christmas, Easter, and feasts during the year. I enjoyed doing this and I would make the arrangements on a Friday or Saturday in the afternoon. One particular afternoon, I was working away in the sacristy, it was for Christmas and I had a lot of arrangements to do. I would bring them out one by one and place them on the altar. Just as I was nearly finished and bringing the last one out, I saw someone in a brown robe with a hood sitting halfway down the aisle. I was taken aback as I knew I had locked all the doors with the church keys. I went back into the sacristy and phoned the ward and asked the attendant to come to the church. He arrived in a few minutes, I told him, "There's someone in the church."

He said, "There could not be. You had to let me in the church was locked."

I said, "Just check the aisles."

He went out, checked all around, and checked the entrance doors, no he said, "There is no one."

I said, "I wasn't imagining it, I saw someone like a monk."

He said, "It must be haunted."

It was very strange, he left as quickly as he arrived, and disappeared.

We always had a lovely live-size crib at Christmas, and the choir, staff with beautiful voices, guitarists and the piano, the patients loved Christmas. A patient robbed the baby Jesus one day when the church was open. We had a fair idea who it was and got the baby Jesus back to his place in the crib before Christmas mass.

At this time, there was a move on from management to move the patients from the lower house approximately four hundred, to various units like Cherry Orchard Hospital, James

Connolly Hospital Blanchardstown, St. Ita's Hospital, St. Loman's Hospital, and some nursing homes. The staff protested because we felt the patients were being well looked after in St Brendan's, but we were informed that the building was no longer fit for purpose and the patients would be better off in more modern units. It apparently was a ministerial order, so the patients were dispersed. The only saving grace was that our unions managed to get a deal where staff who wanted to move to these other areas could go with the patients, and every effort was made to keep the groups of patients in each unit to move together, so their pals would be with them, and a different place would not be such a shock.

The closure of the Lower house with its population of approximately four hundred patients, had a big impact on the general hospitals. Many of our older patients had dementia and were admitted to St. Brendan's because they needed twenty-four-hour nursing care and their relatives could not look after them that was a lot of bed places out of the system at that time. Patients with dementia were spending years in psychiatric hospitals with great care and a homely environment. Now patients with dementia and no relatives to care for them end up spending years in general hospitals when they got physically ill, until nursing home places can be found for them. This was when there was a surge in the construction of private and public nursing homes and a lot of the time, the health board were left footing the bill.

Staff shortages continued with nurses and unions fighting for more staff and being forced into industrial action, including strikes.

This was the gradual beginning of the closure of the hospital; another admission unit in the upper house was to close. Apparently, a dead cat had been left under a prefab extension for weeks, resulting in a ferocious outbreak of fleas. They were everywhere, again the units were evacuated, never to return.

There were a few low-support hostels where patients were living with a nurse calling in to check on them during the day and they were alone at night. It was in one of these low-support hostels that tragedy struck, the Grangegorman murders. I remember driving past the hostel before I turned into the gate of the hospital, there were squad cars there and staff gathered outside. I knew something terrible had happened but we only learned later that day of the tragedy where two ladies were murdered. It was all over the media, "The Grangegorman Murders." I knew all of those ladies well, as two of them had been in the admission unit when I was there. They were gentle souls and did not deserve such a brutal and savage death. The other lady I knew very well, too as she too had spent a lot of time in the admission unit. We were all devastated, as were their relatives. I had been acting ADON (Assistant Director of Nursing) on the night rounds a week before it happened. I would have had to deal with the tragedy, thank god I didn't, as I am sure the nurse, the ADON on that week must have been so shocked calling the Gardaí, ambulance etc. I just hoped she hadn't seen too much, or she would be having nightmares for a long time.

At that time, we had a roster of charge nurses and deputy charges to act as Assistant Director of Nursing, with the permanent Assistant Director of Nursing on night duty. We would check on all the units in the hospital and she would do the community areas. We still had Vergemount, Weir home, Ushers Island, and some hostels. The permanent Assistant

Director of Nursing would return to the hospital after her community rounds and get a report from us if there were any problems outstanding. We always managed to solve problems with the help of the night duty staff. I used to find it a bit nerve-wracking going through the male wards as you could meet a male patient starkers, or they could follow youaround. This would be mainly in the block, the secure unit which was only staffed by male nurses, but the male nurses on duty were very diligent and made sure I was safe.

My next place to work was in a high-support hostel, as part of the overall plan to close St. Brendan's, patients were selected to move out of the hospital to high and low-support hostels. Some of these patients had been through the rehabilitation unit prior to the move to a hostel. These were some of the houses vacated by staff who had occupied them for several years. I was asked as a deputy in rehabilitation to set up and move to one of these hostels. So I went to look at the one I was to set up. It brought back memories to me as I used to babysit for my friend in one of these hostels when I was a student nurse. Some furniture was ordered by the stores department, such as beds and wardrobes. There were to be eight men in this four-bedroomed house, which was formerly inhabited by staff and their families. As soon as nurses who were living in these houses moved out, the HSE kept the houses for hostels. These were the houses on Grangegorman Road called the villas.

It took two weeks to get everything set up and supplies in situ for the opening of this hostel. One day, I had to go to Bargaintown to buy two tables, a dresser, chairs for the dining room, coffee tables etc. One of the care staff said she would come with me. I said great, two heads are better than one. We went into the Bargaintown furniture store on Queen Street and met the manager to discuss what we needed. He showed us around, and my care staff decided she would test out the furniture. She was great, she jumped on the chairs, turned them upside down, same with the tables, coffee tables, to see if everything was strong enough. The manager looked at me in despair.

I said, "She's right, we have some heavy patients." I laughed to myself and thought not much would get past her. In the end, we chose the furniture and left.

On the way back, she said to me, "I hope you didn't think I was being heavy-handed."

I said not at all, "Fair play to you, we don't want rubbish."

Running the hostels was good in some ways, not in others. We now had to do budgets, open accounts for the patients in the post office, budget for the weekly shopping etc. Patients had to pay a small amount of rent. It was like being at home on a bigger scale with eight big children. The daily routine was much the same as the hospital: personnel hygiene, which was difficult with only one bathroom, breakfast, and medication. Some patients attended therapy in the hospital, while others were not able to engage. The house was small and confined to a three-bedroomed. These houses were formerly used for staff who lived there, usually on a temporary basis until they got their own houses, some were two bedroomed, three bedroomed and four bedrooms, and there was a back garden which we used to full potential. It might have seemed like a forward step for management. They could say patients were living in the community, but they were living in hostels staffed day and night with nurses.

At that time, a film crew wanted to shoot some scenes

from the Michael Collins movie, and our old buildings in the hospital, the lower house, were deemed suitable for some of the scenes. The lower house was used where they had installed a tram on cobblestones. Unfortunately the only electricity access was the villas. I was approached by the crew who wanted to run a cable from outside the back of the house, this would be for about three to four weeks. There was great excitement even though there was a lot of disruption at the time, as some of the scenes had to be filmed at dusk. This disrupted the patients in the hospital and the hostels with the noise of gunfire and smoke. It was very loud with explosions for the scenes.

I had been looking for a porta cabin for the garden for our eight patients to use in the evening time. I said if they could drop a properly fitted porta cabin with electricity and a toilet, a darts board and a large colour TV tables and chairs, they could use all the electricity they wanted after all the health board were paying for it and had given the film crew an old creative space to film the scenes. The patients could use this porta cabin as a time out space, as the sitting room in the house was too small. They agreed and did deliver on the deal, the patients were delighted. One particular patient wanted to be in the film, so I had to go with him.

We signed in on a sunny day in July and were given hats and cloaks. He was given a green army outfit, and I had to wear a heavy cloak and a big hat. We were in the scene in front of the GPO, where Devilera was giving a rousing speech. We got the nod to shout, this went on for a few hours. We were hoarse and sweaty as the smoke was in our eyes. When we were finished, we were to leave back the clothes. Johnny did not want to; he wanted to keep the outfit, so I said to him we will slip in our back door and keep the clothes. He was chuffed, and I kept a black hat. It was great when the film crew left, the patients had their outside cabin to enjoy.

I spent two years in that hostel and the staff and I made life as normal as possible for the patients. One of them got a part-time job in a sheltered programme, the remainder of the patients just lived there. They were free to come and go but were still very dependent on staff and most of their routine didn't change. One older patient who needed his bloods taken every six months but point blank refused, even though our two nurses who took all the samples of blood in the hospital and in the hostels, was so nice and persuasive. He still point blanked and refused, he said to me, "You get yours done."

I said, "If I do will you, and you can watch, it's easy."

So I got my samples of blood taken with him watching, and every time I had to do it again, and then he would agree. As a nurse, you would always think, what if that was my father or brother? And you would do whatever you could to persuade them it was safe.

Health and Safety

I was acutely aware of health and safety issues in the hospital for staff and patients. Issues that were not being addressed, I was elected as Health and Safety Officer in 1996. The previous representative had resigned due to a lack of cooperation from management and the constant indifference to health and safety issues. This was another voluntary role with no payment whatsoever and was often seen as interfering in the running of the hospital. My responsibilities were to make representation to the employer on safety, health and welfare matters relating to employees, in the place of work. The intention of consultation is to prevent accidents and ill health, to highlight problems, and to identify means of finding solutions.

I had completed a higher diploma in Health and Safety, and an Instructors Course in manual handling with St. John's Ambulance in Phoenix Park. These two courses were quite time-consuming and difficult to obtain and to pass, however, I managed. I had made several representations to the Health and safety Authority over issues in the hospital. One particular issue was so obvious: inside the front gate, the avenue to the units was full of potholes/craters. Several people had stumbled in them. If you were driving your car, you certainly felt them. I would meet with the Director of Nursing and the hospital administrator on a monthly basis to discuss issues and solutions on health and safety grounds.

I had made several representations and had meetings with the hospital administrator, who seemed to ignore such representations until I actually got an inspector to come out to the hospital one morning. We just managed to catch the administrator as she was leaving her office in the annexe administration building. She got a bit of a shock, but after speaking to him agreed the funds to fix the avenue. There was already a claim in from a patient's relative who had actually fallen and was injured. It was stupid not to fix the obvious instead of waiting until someone claimed compensation.

The next hospital administrator was much more approachable. She was very interested in solving any problems we encountered, of which there were many. The hospital and community areas had not been updated for some time, all of the areas had to be reassessed and plans implemented for maintenance and repairs. Nursing and staff shortages fell under the remit of the hospital management and constant intervention by the unions, which was a continuous effort and had on occasions ended up in a strike situation as a last resort. A lot of time was spent in The Labour Relations, trying to come to some agreement for the best interest of all concerned. This new hospital administrator sent me a thank you letter when I had to resign as health and safety officer when I was assigned as nursing officer to Area 6 in 2,000.

Nurse Education and training

Nurse education and training was held in The Centre of Nurse Education in the hospital. It was a two-story building, with lecture rooms for the different tutors, a practise room where nurses were taught first aid, handling techniques, monitoring blood pressure, temperatures, bedsores, skin conditions, ensuring patient safety if having an epileptic seizure, and many other conditions we might encounter in our daily nursing and observation techniques. We had a photographer and video expert on hand to record different situations that might occur and how we would handle them.

We all did our three years of training in Psychiatric Nursing in the centre of nurse education as was the custom throughout the country, with our theory in two-week sessions four times a year, and the rest of our training was on the wards under the supervision of qualified nurses and charge nurses. We had our curriculum booklet with all the skills we could demonstrate that we had achieved that had to be signed by the charge nurse. This in turn, was examined by the tutors in the school of nursing. We spent a lot of time learning on the job, which was great as we could link the theory with ongoing practice. We soon learned the signs and symptoms of many psychiatric disorders and quite a lot of physical diseases that the patients had.

The nurse education centre was also an ongoing place for in service training for all staff throughout the years, for many courses, Control and restraint, specific techniques for keeping staff and patients safe in violent situations. Counselling courses, rehabilitation, manual handling, and many more. I remember on one refresher course, a nurse who had come to St. Brendan's from St. Pat's to work here. She was so critical of everything in St. Brendan's and giving the speaker a hard time. After several interruptions by her, my friend Teresa stood up and said, "Nobody sent for you to work here; if it's that bad why stay." That shut her up, and she actually stayed until she retired.

The ground floor of the Nurse Education Centre was used for seminars, dances, and patient art exhibitions. There was no degree programme for nurses then, but through lobbying by the tutorial staff and, the unions and nurses themselves, the degree programme for nurses was introduced. Nurses were not deemed to be on the same level of educational status by other disciplines who felt they had not attained a degree. Nurses were to get their degrees in universities all over the country just like any other discipline, such as teachers, social workers, science, technology, etc. Even though nurses in my time had not a degree, they had a Diploma in Nursing which was the highest achievement in nursing at the time, and were registered as psychiatric nurses in my experience, whenever a situation arose on a ward it was not an occupational therapist, social worker, or psychologist that the consultant looked for, it was a nurse.

The degree program for nurses was commenced in 2002, where nurses spent most of their time in universities and had placements in the psychiatric, general, children's hospitals, and community settings. This change was welcomed by the nursing profession, although many nurses found they learned a lot during their placements in hospital and community settings. I think our system was really good as you were learning on the job. When we were qualified, we just did not get degree status at the time, but there were many nurses who did their general nursing, public health nursing, some nurses became tutors, counsellors, instructors in manual handling, first aid, control and restraint, there was no limitation to education. However some of us who got married young, got houses and mortgages and had children, had not the time or the funds to further our education.

Further education was not funded by the health board or the government, so some nurses did their general nursing, children's nursing, intellectual disability, and midwifery at their own expense, and some ventured into the different areas of nursing, but psychiatric nursing was seen as the most challenging and did not suit everyone. Some of us did go on to further education in later years, to degrees, masters, tutors, many of our nurses becoming the tutors for future nurses of all disciplines. I continued with my own education, as did so many of my colleagues.

In 1991- Diploma in Management course with the Royal college of Surgeons.

1992-Women's Affairs courses, -SIPTU Professional College

In 1993- Diploma in Counselling Maynooth College.

In 1997- Rehabilitation course and a certificate in CPR.

In 1998- Diploma in Health, Safety and Welfare at work, University College Dublin.

1998/9 Management Course in manual handling, Ambulances services, St. Mary's Hospital, Phoenix Park.

2000-Evidenced Based Nursing practise, Royal College of Surgeons

2003/04- Assistant Directors Leadership Development Course -Institute of Public Administration

2004 -Bachelor of Nursing Science -Dublin City University

2006 -Masters in Nursing and Healthcare -Dublin City University

I was a member of the SIPTU Committee who were excellent at providing workshops and training, and had excellent presentations and speakers at our annual conferences throughout the country. The current Minister for Health each year would come to the conference and give a speech, sometimes they were warmly greeted, sometimes they were questioned about what they intended to do about the state of the health service.

The Minister for Health, who at the time was Charlie Haughey in 1997, visited the lower house. I was on duty in Unit B. He did the usual tour and greetings, he stopped to ask me how things were. I said the patients are well looked after, this is their home, it's such a pity it's in much need of proper maintenance.

He said, "What do you mean?" I brought him into the kitchen, much to the surprise for Mary, one of our great household staff, who was making tea for the patients. I said just look up at the ceiling the paint is flaking off it. It's the same in a lot of units, they are only painted every eight to ten years, and all of the other maintenance necessities were attended to as emergencies as they happened. He said he would see what he could do, I said thanks but took it with a grain of salt.

The following year, we got new windows in the lower house. I just said to myself that's a sure sign they are going to close it, and it was a few years later. Discussions began about the availability of beds in other hospitals and nursing homes.

In 1983, we started a variety group, this was great for staff morale. We needed something at that time to lift our spirits from the ongoing staff shortages, budget restraints, and lack of services. There was great interest and excitement in the group. It involved all staff, anyone with a talent or willing to lend a hand in the group. We needed singers, actors, dancers, comedians, all sorts of people. We also needed backstage staff, electricians, porters, carpenters, painters, make-up artists, costume staff, sound systems and technicians, choreographers, and transport staff for shows outside the hospital.

There was a great buzz around the hospital with many tea breaks spent getting costumes and the stage ready for the shows. My part in the variety group was to paint the scenes for the props for each different show, we used gallons of paint until it was right. I had a lot of experience and practice doing paintings around the hospital, I used to paint all the windows in some units for Christmas for several years, and the patients loved them. We did many musicals, Showboat, Westside Story, The Meaning of Life etc. We had very talented people on the staff, some singers, dancers, and the comedians P.J and John, who entertained us with their various sketches. They were well written and sometimes an opportunity to hit a nerve with management, but they got away with it. After all it was a comedy sketch.

After several and many rehearsals, we entered the "Tops

of the Town" competition, scoring in the top five many times, and once we got to the semi-final. It took a lot of effort transporting props, costumes, and equipment, but everyone pulled together for the good of the show.

My good friend and I did the make-up for our actors and singers before going on stage. I still have the make-up box since the shows finished, the make-up was hard to remove, and several bottles of castor oil were used after each show. Every year, we would raise funds for different causes: The Mental Association, Cancer, brain injury. One year, one cause we donated to was the sudden infant death syndrome or cot death because of our Laura, it was a pity it had to end, but nurses were emigrating, staff were moving to different areas, so we had to finish.

St. Brendans Hospital
Variety Group
Presents

"My Kinda People"

In Aid of

Schizophrenia Ireland.

(Great Wall of China Trek)

PROGRAMME

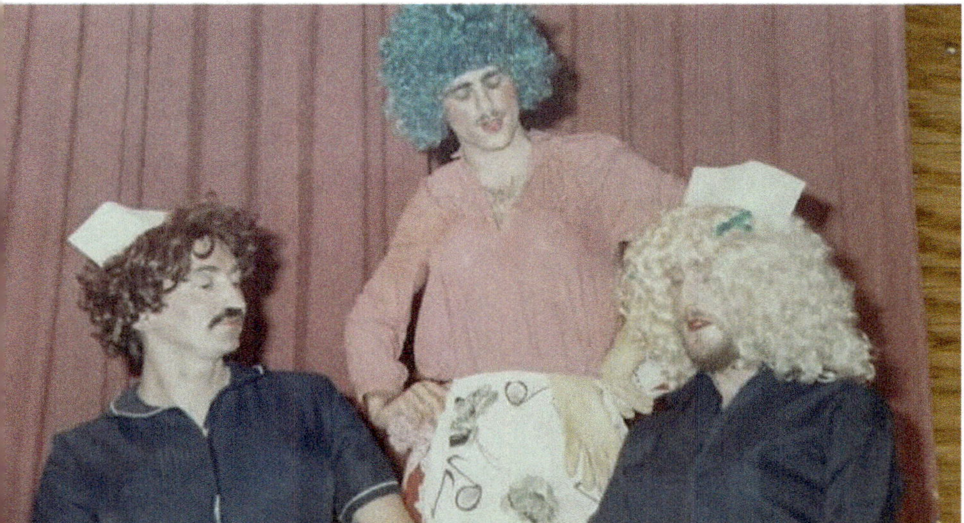

Some of the scenes from the various performances

STATUE
FOR

SAINT
BRENDAN'S 6^{D}
MAGAZINE

VOLUME 2. NUMBER 5. APRIL, 1968

Pictures of some actors, singers and people who visited the hospital in previous years

THE

CANDID CAMERA

OF PHOTOGRAPHER J. LEDWIDGE

TRIED TO CATCH

MINNIE, BATTY & NOEL PURCELL UNAWARES

BUT BATTY FOOLED HIM!

SAINT BRENDAN'S MAGAZINE

6D

DICKIE ROCK

VOLUME 1 NUMBER 10. AUGUST 1967

GATEWAY
4p
MARCH

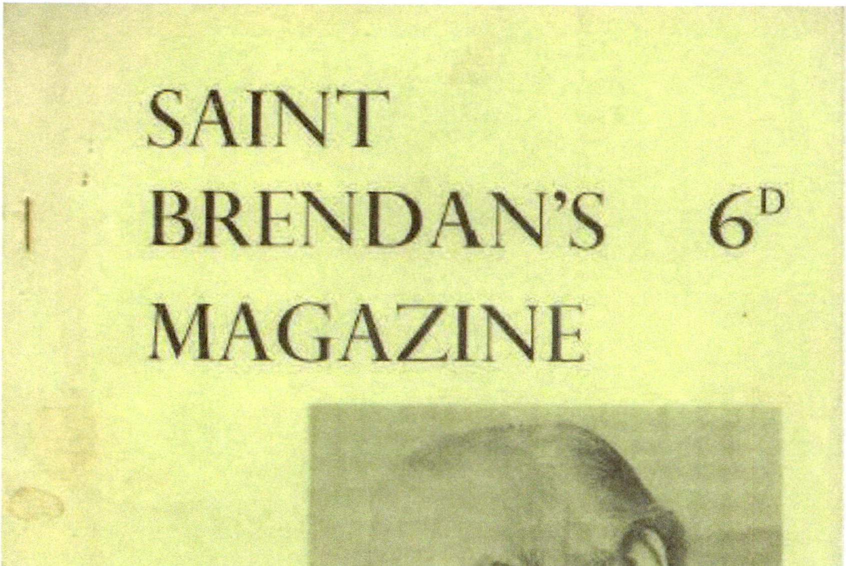
SAINT
BRENDAN'S 6D
MAGAZINE

CECIL
SHERIDAN

VOLUME 1. NUMBER 9. JULY 1967

GATEWAY

MARCH APRIL

Improvements in Psychiatry and Intellectual disability services in the 50s, 60s, 70s, 80s, and 90s. Improvements in St. Brendan's, St. Loman's, and St. Ita's happened in the late sixties, seventies, eighties, and nineties, all three hospitals were considered together in alleviating the overcrowding in St. Brendan's. In 1961,170 female patients were transferred to St. Loman's, and in 1963, an Autistic unit was built in St. Loman's for children and young adults run by Dr Crotty and staff. Under Dr Crotty's guidance patients participated in working in the kitchens, offices the, dining rooms, and some wards as they had done in St Brendan's, the difference being that in St. Loman's, they wore their own clothes, were encouraged to be as independent as they could, look after their own appearance going to the hairdresser and beauticians, and lived in a homely environment, some patients even went out to work and returned to the hospital in the evenings. They had their own committees who ran dances, bingo, etc., at which relatives and visitors could attend. Unfortunately, Dr Crotty died in 1964, and Dr Ivor Browne took over until his appointment to St. Brendan's in 1966, following the retirement of Dr Dunne in 1965. St. Loman's continued to develop outpatient clinics, day hospitals, and community services.

There were suggestions by government ministers that all of the older patients should be transferred to county homes at a lower cost to the state. The first place looked at in 1857 was in Wicklow, St Colman's Hospital Rathdrum. Dr Dunne visited it and reported that the newly built sanatorium was good, but the rest of the hospital was deplorable. There were no sanitary conditions in the wards, the patients were being washed in tubs, some of the walls had holes in them, and the heating was non-existent. For the next fifty years, plans were proposed for over half a century by Dr Francis White, Dr Connolly Norman, and Dr John Dunne. Plans that were proposed and rejected.

The usual problem was money and finding the cheapest way to house the lunatics of Ireland. In 1858, the board agreed to take over a former T.B. hospital in Crooksling at the foot of the Dublin Mountains, which had been set up by Dr Noel Browne in the time T.B. was rampant. He believed that patients with T.B. needed fresh air as well as medical treatment, so patients were wheeled out onto the verandas of the ward each day. 200 elderly patients from St. Brendan's were transferred there. This reduced the number of patients in St. Brendan's to 1,800, but the longstanding problem of overcrowding remained. In 1959, at long last, the financial position of the board had improved, and permission was given for the upgrading of the existing buildings and some temporary buildings unfit for human habitation were removed. In 1960, 150 geriatric patients were transferred to St. Mary's Phoenix Park, this further relieved the overcrowding.

Conditions also improved for nurses in the 60s, nurses were no longer expected to work in the kitchens, laundries, and stores. Dr Dunne advocated that working in these areas were essential for patients for therapy and purpose for their day, and that nurses needed to be supervising patients, lay people had not the training to react if a patient became anxious, violent, or withdrawn. Nurses continued to supervise patients only where they worked as in the laundry and industrial therapies. In 1966, the bakeries in St Itas and St. Brendan's closed. When I started nursing in 1972, nurses were still supervising patients in these areas, and it was important as it allowed patients to be occupied under the supervision of nurses.

Professor Ivor Browne, who was appointed RMS in 1966, advocated for the therapeutic treatment of the patients in the hospital and in the community, services were not progressing, which left ongoing overcrowding in buildings which were old with inadequate utility services, no therapeutic activities, low staff morale. Recruitment and training of psychiatric staff hampered the development of services both in the hospital and the community. He wanted to raise the public's image of the psychiatric service in Dublin. Each psychiatric team would serve its own catchment area from hospital to community and domiciliary services following the patients' discharge, an integrated system. In the latter part of the sixties, psychiatric teams were strengthened with the appointments of psychologists, psychiatric social workers, occupational therapists, and art therapy. Programmes to stimulate chronic patients, some of whom were mentally handicapped. A well-known variety artist, Ben Bono was appointed as a recreational officer to coordinate social and recreational activities. Nurses were expected to take part in these programmes, but rarely did nurses get the opportunity as they had their nursing duties as well.

Dr Browne had advocated for "The Brendan Project" where two acres of land in St. Brendan's would be set aside to build a major resource centre that would give access to those "at risk," "revolving door" and ex-patients the skills and education to take responsibility for their own lives in the community, and to prepare for open employment or specific educational training. The project group had involvement from medicine, psychology, education, sociology, communications, art, drama, and vocational training, working on the "Re socialization Project" for the most disadvantaged human beings in our society, which were the long stay patients. This project had been approved by the government, then a new programme manager had been appointed with the brief to close down the hospital. He continued to close units and move patients as described despite objections from medical, nursing, and auxiliary staff.

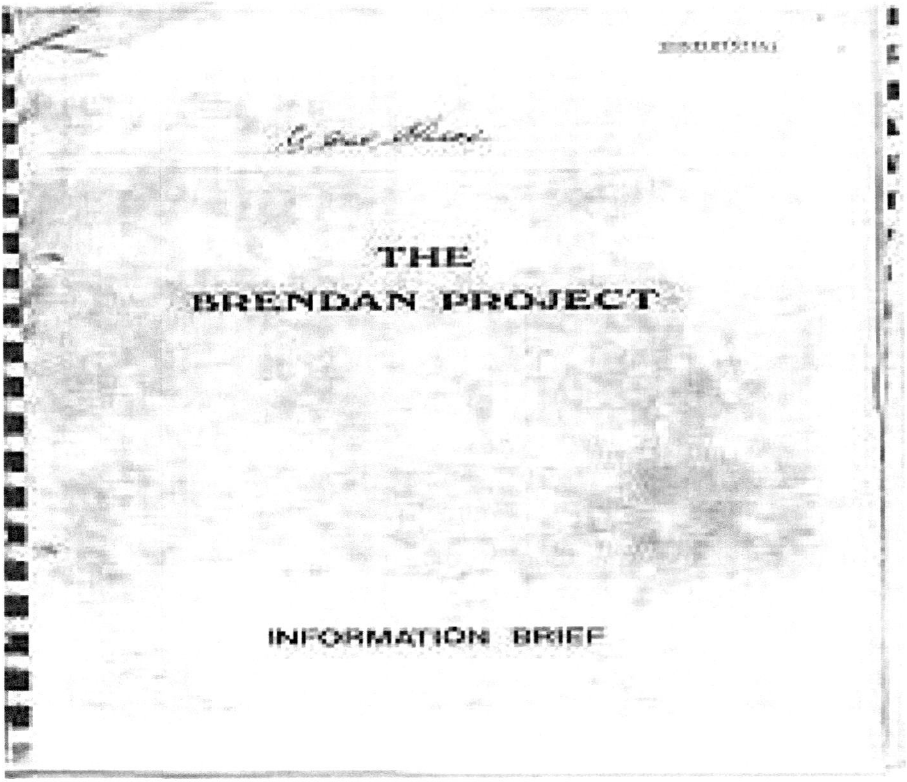
THE
BRENDAN PROJECT

INFORMATION BRIEF

Every couple of years, there was movement in the hospital and hostels, where charge nurses and deputy charge nurses were moved to different wards. This was at the discretion of the Director of Nursing in St Brendan's, where there was no choice given, as to what area or ward you would like to relocate. It was different in other hospitals like St Ita's in Portrane, where charges and deputies were invited to give their preferences, but we just had to go where we were assigned to. It was a shock or a surprise as to where you were sent, I never expected to be moved to a different service. On the day of the changes, you got your brown envelope with your assignment. My next assignment was to work in Area Six, which looked after the catchment area of Clonsilla, Blanchardstown, parts of Finglas, and hostels and day centres in that area. Nurses had opted to work in that area in recent years, at that time, as it suited them to be nearer home and for various other reasons. I was a bit shocked to be moved out of St Brendan's as I had spent nearly twenty five years there, and I loved working there, area six was still under the umbrella services of St Brendan's, just different staff and management. I just had to get on with it and get to know a whole different service and colleagues, doctors, nurses and other various disciplines. I was sent to a large hostel in Area Six, "Daneswood."

Area Six

This service was largely community-based, with some high and low-support hostels, day centres, outpatient clinics and an acute unit in Blanchardstown. I already knew some of the staff who had previously voluntarily moved from St Brendan's. I was assigned to a large hostel in Glasnevin, Daneswood. It was a beautiful red, bricked large house with male and female residents. I was also to oversee two low-support hostels, which were staffed by housekeepers at night and community nurse input during the day. Some had been living there for years as they were not deemed suitable for independent living. This house I was assigned to and its residents needed an overhaul, as it too had been previously run by a housekeeper, so when the nurses moved in naturally, there was conflict. Luckily, when I arrived, the nurses were in charge as the housekeeper had retired.

I decided to see what was available to these residents in the community. They attended a day centre daily and were collected by a minibus each morning and returned each evening. There was no direct bus to the day centre. I would call the day centre during the day when I sorted out administrative issues in the house and the low-support hostels. I had learned from my previous experience in the hostels in St Brendan's of services and entitlements for example, clothes and shoe allowance, dental, and optical treatments.

I gradually got to know these residents, their needs, entitlements, their relatives, habits, likes and dislikes. Most of these residents were there a long time as there was nowhere else for them to progress too. The gardens in this house were quite extensive, and the residents enjoyed sitting out any fine evening.

We arranged barbecues, which they really enjoyed and took part in the cooking, had a beer, and life had some normality for them. They went to a day centre every day, nine to five, which got them out of the house and engaged in activities in the day centre. There was a variety of activities such as candle making, bingo, arts, and crafts etc. It made their life seem normal as if they were going to work and got them out of the house.

One of these patients was a ward of court but did not benefit from all the money he had. He was surviving with limited clothes, no personal belongings, etc that he was entitled to. I decided to contact his solicitor and ask why he had no personal belongings with all the wealth he was entitled to. The solicitor said he never asked for anything, it had been three years since he had contacted him. I told the solicitor he needed clothes, a radio, etc. The solicitor said he could not bring him out to get any of these things.

I said, "I'll make a list of what he wants and send it to you."

So eventually, he got back to us and informed us to get what the patient wanted, and send him receipts. We got him everything he asked for and sent off receipts. I told the solicitor to give him an annual sum of money for his own use. He was delighted, so an agreement was put in place for him. He had no one to vouch for him. I told him this was sorted, and he could have new clothes, etc., every year, gave him his solicitor's name and details.

The gardens needed an overhaul and I approached the Botanic garden supervisor for help. I suggested it could be a project for the agricultural students. They agreed and the students drew up three proposals after spending a few evenings mapping out the garden and the seating areas. And I had asked them to incorporate an exercise space where we could have a covered pool table that could double up as a table tennis table. The residents spent a lot of time in the garden in the evenings after their tea when they returned from the day centre. We asked for sensory plants and calming plants, which would help these patients relax from the beautiful aromas and the textures of the plants, as one of our residents had poor sight and used to feel the texture of things. I applied for funding through the national lottery, and we were granted a few thousand euros. We eventually picked one of the plans after consultation with the residents. After much debating between themselves and the staff, we all agreed on one of the plans to enhance the garden into a sensory garden, with exercise space and seating areas.

Shortly after that, however I was informed by my Director of Nursing that I was to be promoted to acting Assistant Director of Nursing in St Ita's hospital. I was flabbergasted, as I was not expecting to have to move to St Itas, as some nurses referred to as the peninsula, I just remembered all of the nurses that were sent there for punishment on the blue bus. I wanted to finish the plans we had for the high support hostel as the residents were keen, and it would greatly enhance their recreational space, and the sensory gardens would have such a calming effect for them if they or the staff were having a bad day. Unfortunately I had to hand over the plans to the next person to take charge of the hostel.

I got a phone call from the Director of Nursing in St Ita's to come out for a meeting that week. I was not expecting to have to leave so quickly. He wanted me to start immediately, but I said I had to finish up properly in my current role and do a proper handover to the next Clinical Nurse Manager. He agreed to give me another week.

My Director of Nursing said, "I had better go as I was next in line for promotion, and if I refused, I would miss the chance. The next person on the list would be offered the place." My Director of Nursing and the staff arranged a going away evening for me, as was customary when anyone was leaving the service. It was a nice evening with a meal and a few drinks and a present. I was delighted and surprised. Most of the staff in Area Six had worked in St Brendan's prior to this, so I knew them all well. I was quite apprehensive about going to St Ita's even though it was nearer to where I lived, and the traffic in the mornings was getting worse by the day going to my present job. I only knew two people in St Ita's at that time, the charge nurse who had come to St Brendan's for a year to the admission unit where I was deputy charge and another nurse who was the daughter of my dad's friend and was in the union and worked representing staff for years.

I had spent so long in St Brendan's and Area Six thirty years it was hard to leave, but maybe it was time for a change, and generally nurses working in Psychiatric hospitals face the same challenges in every part of the country, but I think Dublin hospitals and hospitals in other big cities receive more volumes of patients due to urban population. So I said goodbye to St Brendan's, which I loved and set forth for my next ten years in St Ita's, but that's another story, it was another step in my life in Psychiatry.

Access to Psychiatric Services

Access to psychiatric services in the last hundred years was completely different to how it works today. In 1815, when Grangegorman Lunatic Asylum opened for admissions, and in many of the other psychiatric hospitals throughout the country, the procedure was unregulated and many patients or lunatics as they were referred to then, often had no say in their admission. Patients were admitted for many reasons and not all because they had mental health problem. Some patients were admitted from the workhouse as they had nowhere else to go, some unmarried mothers were admitted from the railway union where mothers had a short stay before their babies were taken from them for adoption, some from mother and baby homes, men who were homeless, young men who had spent time in industrial schools and had then been farmed out to work on the land, which did not always work out and the next port of call if they were disagreeable was the psychiatric hospitals. Other patients were admitted over land or property where a relative had them committed even though they had no psychiatric problems. So many people were confined to the asylum for the rest of their lives, for some it was a place of asylum, even though they were treated appallingly in the early days, they had shelter, food, treatments were experimental, and some barbaric, gradually things started to improve very slowly. There were so many displaced people in Psychiatric hospitals. Consultants and physicians would travel abroad exploring how other countries, many of their populations of people with mental health problems, come back to Ireland and instigate some therapies and treatments they had learned about.

When I started my training in psychiatry in 1972, admissions were still difficult. Admissions were voluntary, temporary and person of unsound mind (PUM). Voluntary admissions were where the person signed themselves in for treatment, temporary where a relative and G.P. would sign the person, or if there was no relative, the Gardaí or specific judiciary could sign the person in. In the case of PUM, a person might be brought in by the Gardaí, or the hospital would send out a nurse escort to the person's house or premises to escort the person to the hospital via ambulance or Gardaí escort accompanying the nurses. I was sent out on many escorts with another nurse, one such escort, and we were locked in a house in Finglas for four hours. The patient was totally paranoid and elated, no matter how we tried to persuade her there was no talking to her. Eventually, she let me use the phone, no mobiles at that time, to take her husband away. I was ringing the guards for three hours before they came to assist us. Another time, I was sent to Rathmines with another nurse, the patient created such a scene the whole street was out watching, again, the guards had to assist us. I was on night duty another night, sent on escort for an alcoholic lady to the flats, up three flights of stairs, no lifts at that time. Two ambulance men came with us with a stretcher, when we got to her door, it was open, she was conked out, and so we just lifted her onto the stretcher and brought her back to the hospital. I am sure my colleagues have many more stories regarding escorts. The escorts by nurses stopped when three male nurses from St Ita's Hospital got stabbed and were seriously injured in the assault by the patient. Thankfully, they recovered in time, but no nurse expects to be assaulted and injured during their days' work.

Now, these types of escorts are well organized by the Assisted Admissions Team, in conjunction with the relevant community nurses, the G.P., the Gardaí, the consultant psychiatrist, all forms have to be signed and completed and sent to the relevant hospital prior to the escort so everything can be put in place to get the patient safely to the hospital.

Psychiatric services can still be difficult for people to access quickly your G.P. might be the first avenue who may provide support directly or refer you to the H.S.E community mental health team. This team provides services for all ages, including adult mental health services, child and adolescent mental health services, and psychiatry for later life services. Community services are available Monday to Friday in outpatient clinics, day hospitals, and day centres, with community mental health nurses on at the weekend, like public health nurses for people who need ongoing monitoring and services. The community mental health team comprises of psychiatrists, mental health nurses, psychologists, family therapists, social workers, child care workers, speech and language therapists, occupational therapists, and counselling services.

When Service users require in-patient treatment, this will be provided in a psychiatric unit, some of these units are attached to general hospitals, depending on what part of the country you live in. These admissions may be voluntary where a person seeks help and may be admitted from an outpatient clinic if the person's mental state has deteriorated, or the service user may end up in accident and emergency departments, with referral to the psychiatric registrar on call, who will assess the service user who may need admission. Some admissions may be involuntary, where a service user may be a danger to themselves or others. The Mental Health Act 2001 sets out provisions and principles that apply to anyone who is admitted involuntarily.

Sometimes, if you are referred to a psychiatrist or mental health professional, there may be a waiting time, depending on the service in your area. This happens too with physically ill service users in the community, who end up in Accident and Emergency departments with acute illnesses or accidents.

There is still a stigma attached to mental or psychological problems. If you go to the Accident and Emergency departments with a broken leg, heart attack, stroke or other issues, many of the visible signs are evident, but when a person presents with mental health problems, they may look normal to everyone else, you cannot see the inner torture, the anxiety, the fear, the isolation, the depression, the suicidal ideation, the loneliness and despair. So, as the saying goes, "Do not judge the book by its cover," look inside the pages to get to the truth and hopefully be in a position to help someone in their darkest hour.

There appears to be a notion in government departments that people only get physically or psychiatrically unwell during the week and not at weekends, bank holidays, Christmas and other times during the year. All services should be available 24/7, and working in the health services, and indeed many other essential services, should be recognized and funded appropriately by those ministers running the country. There have been great improvements in the treatment of mental health issues. The awareness is growing. It affects everyone, rich or poor, old or young. Remember you could be that service user someday, so treat everyone like you would like to be treated.

So, in 2013, St Brendan's hospital was closed, and a new unit opened on the north circular road called "The Phoenix Unit" to house the remaining patients. It is a state-of-the-art unit with modern facilities. The Dublin institute of Technology now stands on the grounds of the former hospital, some of the buildings and the churches remain, but like when I started my career in Psychiatric nursing you would need a map to get around it, and they have wonderful facilities for all of the students, staff and visitors, it's great to see, but for those of us who worked there we will always have great memories.

Carers

Carers who look after their loved ones at home with dementia or physical or depilating illnesses, and those carers who look after their children with love and dedication for them often at the expense of their own lives. Carers who have devoted their lives and careers to do this get some or little help from the government. Carers allowance is still means tested and more often than not people are not entitled to it even though they are saving the government billions each year. Carers look after their loved ones not for monetary gain but out of love, it's high time this service was recognised

Pictures from the past of colleagues and events in the hospital from the gateway and hospital magazines.

A HAPPY NEW YEAR

TO ALL OUR

READERS

JAN - FEB 1973

GATEWAY

CHRISTMAS 1972

6TH ANNIVERSARY EDITION

GATEWAY

5p

GATEWAY
NEW YEAR 1970

Gateway
4p
APRIL

Lady

Gateway
JULY
AUGUST

Gateway

1974
GATEWAY

GATEWAY
Christmas
1969

1969

GATEWAY

ST. BRENDAN'S MAGAZINE

SAINT BRENDAN'S MAGAZINE

6D

VOLUME 2. NUMBER 8. JUNE, 1968

SAINT BRENDAN'S MAGAZINE
CHRISTMAS EDITION
1966

SAINT BRENDAN'S MAGAZINE

SEPTEMBER 1968

Patients' Poems

Life Story

My life story is very hard to write,
I found that out one day
But now I'm going to try it
Only in a different way.

Let's start at the beginning
I'm an orphan as you know
But god is very good to me
No matter where I go.

When i was a baby
God called my mum away
And then my auntie took me
To rear me day to day.

I had three sisters that time
But he only left me one,
And then he called my dad away
So now I'm left with none

I'm not looking for sympathy
For that's something I don't take
I'd rather get a cup of tea

Now I'm going to doctors
Nearly every single day
And though they try they cannot
Ever take the pain away

My aunt and uncle I so loved
For being so kind to me
The day came too for them to go,
And say good-bye to me.

That started all my trouble
Because now I'm all alone
With nobody to greet me
Whenever I go home.

But I still have one true friend,
To help me when I'm ill
When I ask her to take me home
She always says I will.

I tell her all my troubles
And she's sure to solve them all
But I'll have to repay her

And a little bit of cake
First time we went to Co Clare,
My auntie brought us there
We had such a nice holiday
I wanted to stay there.

But I was young and healthy then
And knew no ache nor pain,
So now I often sit and wish
I had those days again.

If I ever get that haul.
But friends like that are very scarce
They all want you when you're well
And if you want to prove this
Get sick and you will tell.

This poem is nearly finished
And I hope it's not too long
So I'll send you the magazine
Before they say it's gone

MUSIC

Music of the mind
brings with it a beauty of
an aestetic kind
and with it a longing
where in holiness you find
the happiness of the soul
of the purest kind.
It brings you sweet contentment
with peace of mind and will.
It takes away resentment
then purity will fill.
The beauty of the phrases
shows how you love
the one on whom the praises
are shining from above.

P. McG.
Unit 9.

IT'S GREAT TO BE ALIVE!

Another day has come and gone
And though it did deprive
Another day from my life's span;
It's great to be alive!

I look around this comely land
And see the plantings thrive,
I see God's hand in everything;
It's great to be alive!

God's greatest gift to us is Time,
Our sins that we may shrive,
I thank Him now with all my heart;
It's great to be alive!

Rain and cloud oftimes depress,
But when sunshine does arrive,
We laugh and sing all day long;
It's great to be alive!

Pain and illness, strife and woe,
No matter what they connive,
We destroy them if we think -
It's great to be alive!

Seeing children at their play,
Like bees within the hive
Busy with their little worlds;
It's great to be alive!

And though my bus is always late,
Ten minutes or maybe five,
After I curse and swear a bit;
It's great to be alive!

So let nothing daunt life's journey,
Do your best and always strive,
When you reach the end you'll say -
'Twas great to be alive!

Anon.

...ational Neurosis?)

In this land of topsy-turveydom
That's called the Emerald Isle
My 'rest cure' in St. Brendan's
Is just another weary trial.

A hospital is for the sick,
Or so I've always understood,
But here I'm just a patient
And so my name is Mud.

There's rules and regulations
By the dozen and the score,
But they're not designed to help the sick,
Whose hearts and minds are sore.

Oh, no! In dear old Gorman's Grange
The patient matters least,
She's just a nuisance round the house,
Half criminal, half beast.

Without Grangegorman's captives,
Giving others jobs galore,
The rate of jailers unemployed
Would very quickly soar.

But appearances must be kept up,
And so the Golden Rule
Is, tell the patient she's to blame,
Because she's just a fool.

Yet some year soon the scene will change
And us despised will laugh;
There will be so many patients
That there won't be any staff !

<u>Nora Purcell</u>

OH! ME NERVES!

I've got browned-off with this talk of depression,
Let's make '69 bright and free,
One would think we were still under Vicky,
With this long-winded whine of "Poor Me!".

Our forbears are dead but not buried,
Their timidities stay with us still:
"I daren't", "You can't", "No, we mustn't",
With an atmosphere dreary and chill.

Well, I got annoyed with repression,
I spat on my hands and I fought
For the right to be cheerful and happy,
Whatever the Puritans thought.

I kissed all the lads I could corner,
I drank all the wine I could hold,
I tackled the jobs left by shirkers,
And walloped the bullying scold.

I changed jobs without thought of the morrow,
I took what I got with a smile,
I made use of my elders' left-overs
And fashioned my own sort of style.

I wore slacks that raised prudish eyebrows,
I told naughty stories and bold,
I left the mollycoddles to swelter,
And sought for air fresh and cold.

I got rid of "me nerves" in the process,
And fed all the pills to the pup;
And as for my nagging preceptress:
"You're a pest, Great-Aunt-Sarah*, Shut Up".

[illegible]

7

BIRTHDAY

Thirty-one candles on the little
cake,
and just herself and I.
It would be too embarrassing
to sing "Happy Birthday" by
herself, she said
when she had turned the light off,
but that she felt like crying,
and then laughed.

And for a moment, every light a year
a gentle lonely witness
lit the darkened room of one man's life.
Infant candles, boy candles, man candles,
all one glow.
Not years any longer, but a life; not
notes, but a deep quiet cord.

Being twenty-one is an unmixed blessing!
But suddenly to have grown up entirely
can be quite as wistful as the whisper
of a tiny candle,
or the silence of a song too embarrassing
to be sung
by one's flickering sweetheart, in the
corner of the eye
of a darkened room.

D.D.

DUBLIN
BRANCH

About the Author

My name is Lucy Walshe, I live in Dublin Ireland, and I spent thirty years working in the largest psychiatric hospital in Dublin. I am married with four adult children and seven grandchildren. I met my husband in the hospital when I started work there at eighteen years of age, we were together fifty years, and he too was a psychiatric nurse. My dear husband passed away last year November 2023. Retired now for a few years I wrote this book to enlighten people about mental illness, treatments used and improvements for patients and staff today. The experience I gained in Grangegorman was unimaginable, as people were admitted for all sorts of reasons as well as those who were actually mentally ill. I spent my life there and gained many lasting friendships with colleagues through good times and bad, we were like a family in a big campus and still support each other.

Printed in Great Britain
by Amazon

57151025R00155